Authority MC/103/181/C Labour Schedule

BRITISH VISA
BRITISH CONSULATE GENERAL,
KOBE. JAPAN.

No. 16289   Date 30th June, 1941.

Valid for travel to

Palestine

Single journey only.

The Valid until 30th Sept, 1941.

Period of stay at discretion of
Immigration authority.

BRITISH PRO-CONSUL

CONSULAT GENERAL
D'EGYPTE A TOKIO

Visa

No. 130

Durée de la validité

Validité { Pour un seul voyage.
Pour tous les voyages
effectués pendant la
durée de la validité

Droits payés   Yen 3,40

Le Consul Général

J. Simaika

FEB 21 2002

CONSULAR SERVICE
30 JUN 41
KOBE

The visa for Palestine No. 16289 issued
at the British Consulate-General, Kobe,
on the 30th June 1941, is hereby extended
valid for the journey to Palestine until
31st December, 1941.

BRITISH PRO-CONSUL

BRITISH CONSULATE GENERAL
16 AUG 41
KOBE

CONSULAR SERVICE

BRITISH TRANSIT VISA.
H.B.M. CONSULATE GENERAL,
KOBE, JAPAN.

No. 16358   Date 22nd July, 1941.

Valid for the sole
purpose of unavoidable
transit through

British India and Ceylon
on a direct journey to

Palestine

Period of stay.

Single journey only

Date of

Various

IMMIGRATION DEPARTMENT
STRAITS SETTLEMENTS

Taca Hersz-Persich

No 1180

Le Consulat des Pays-Bas à Kaunas déclare par la présente que pour l'admission d'étrangers au Surinam, au Curaçao et autres possessions néerlandaises en Amérique un visa d'entrée n'est pas ~~necess~~ requis.

Kaunas, le 27 juillet 1940

Zwartendijk

Consul des Pays-Bas ai

CONSULAAT DER NEDERLANDEN KAUNAS

TRANSIT VISA.

Seen for the journey through Japan (to Suranam, Curaçao and other Netherlands' colonies.)

1940 VII. 31.

Consul du Japon à Kaunas.

CONSULAT DU JAPON KAUNAS LITHUANIE 在カウナス大日本帝國領事館

在カウナス 領事代理 杉原千畝

昭和十五年七月三十一日

滞在拾日間

敦賀上陸

本名ハ行先地ノ査証ヲ有スルモ本邦通過ニ必要ナル現金ヲ有セス且ツ乗船券ノ予約ナキ者ニ付キ在神戸猶太人協會ノ保証ヲ徴シ通過特許セリ

通過特許 昭和16年3月14日ヨリ向フ十四日間有効 福井縣

入國特許 自昭和16年3月28日 至昭和16年5月26日 兵庫縣

出國許可 署第202號

出國期限 昭和16年8月23日迄

經由 神戸 上海 向

兵庫縣

... September, 1941. 16

Shanghai. 6 ...

for Passport Control Officer.

BRITISH CONSULATE GENERAL SHANGHAI

...ED TO REPORT TO ALIENS DEPARTMENT ... L BAZAR, CALCUTTA ... N 24 HOURS.

DATE 13/9/...

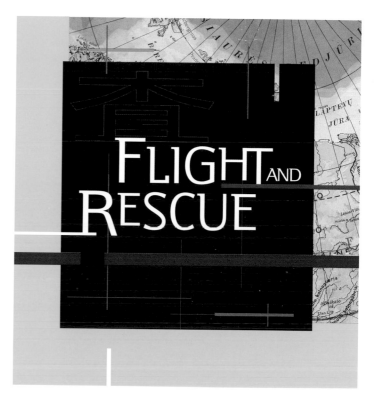

FLIGHT AND RESCUE

UNITED
STATES
HOLOCAUST
MEMORIAL
MUSEUM

WASHINGTON, D.C.

The publication of this volume was made possible by the support of the
Harry and Jeanette Weinberg Foundation, Baltimore, Maryland.

Published in association with the exhibition *Flight and Rescue,*
held at the United States Holocaust Memorial Museum,
Washington, D.C., May 4, 2000, to October 21, 2001.

Project Director: Stephen Goodell
Principal Authors: Susan Bachrach, Anita Kassof
Editor: Edward Phillips

Publications Director: Mel Hecker
Production Editor: Mariah Keller
Art Director: Lea Sesardic
Production Manager: Dwight Bennett

Editorial Assistance: Dieter Kuntz
Photographic Coordination: Satu Haase-Webb
Research and Project Assistance: Clare Cronin, Neal Guthrie,
Paul Rose, Laura Surwit

Object Photography: Max Reid (USA), Shigefumi Kato, Hiromi
Ohgi, Osamu Wantanabe (Japan), Kestutis Stoškus (Lithuania)

Designed by: Inglis Design, Galesville, Maryland

Typeset in Monotype Janson, Jeunesse, and Trade Gothic
by Duke & Company, Devon, Pennsylvania

Printed by: Palace Press, Inc.

PRINTED IN CHINA

First Edition

Library of Congress Cataloging-in-Publication Data

United States Holocaust Memorial Museum.
Flight and rescue / United States Holocaust Memorial Museum.
    p.   cm.
Published in association with the exhibition *Flight and Rescue,*
held at the United States Holocaust Memorial Museum,
Washington, D.C., May 4, 2000, to October 21, 2001.
Includes bibliographical references (p.) and index.
ISBN 0-89604-704-0 (cloth)

1. Refugees, Jewish—Lithuania—Exhibitions. 2. World War,
1939–1945—Jews—Lithuania—Exhibitions. 3. Jews—
Persecutions—Lithuania—Exhibitions. 4. World War,
1939–1945—Jews—Rescue—Lithuania. 5. Lithuania—Ethnic
relations—Exhibitions. 6. World War, 1939–1945—Jews—
Soviet Union—Exhibitions. 7. Jews—Persecutions—Soviet
Union—Exhibitions. 8. Refugees, Jewish—Soviet Union—
Exhibitions. 9. Soviet Union—Ethnic relations. 10. World War,
1939–1945—Jews—Rescue—Japan—Exhibitions.
11. Refugees, Jewish—Japan—Exhibitions. I. Title.
DS135.L5 U68 2000
362.87'81'08992404793—dc21   00-011394
                                                          CIP

Cover, map: Hanni Sondheimer Vogelweid, California
Endpapers: Henry Taca, Florida
Frontispiece and Contents: Photographs by Toru Kono. Private
Collection, Courtesy of Osaka City Museum of Modern Art

CONTENTS

ACKNOWLEDGMENTS

Making comprehensible the staggering proportions of the Holocaust is one of the primary objectives of the United States Holocaust Memorial Museum. Since its opening in 1993, the Museum has developed a host of programs, publications, and exhibitions in an ongoing effort to explain the significance of this cataclysmic event. The research behind these projects often brings together details that unfold the intricate layers of Holocaust history and memory. Most powerful are the personal stories about individual lives, which can illuminate in unexpected ways the catastrophe that was the Holocaust. Such was the case with *Flight and Rescue*—a project that evolved over a six-year period.

In 1994, during the development of a major exhibition about the Kovno ghetto in Lithuania, Founding Director Jeshajahu "Shaike" Weinberg thought it would be important to develop a small, complementary display on Chiune Sugihara, the Japanese acting consul posted to that Baltic nation at the beginning of the war. In 1940 Sugihara had liberally provided transit visas that made escape from war-torn eastern Europe possible for some 2,000 Polish Jews mere months before the genocidal phase of the Holocaust began in the summer of 1941. A request by his government led Sugihara to document the names of people to whom he had issued visas. The Museum found this remarkable 31-page list of 2,140 names in the "Jewish Problem Files" at the Japanese Foreign Ministry Diplomatic Record Office in Tokyo.

Also in 1994, Leo Melamed, a member of the Museum's governing board, the United States Holocaust Memorial Council, loaned the Museum a Polish passport with the Sugihara visa stamped inside. As a child, Leo had accompanied his parents on the long odyssey to safety that began with their flight to Lithuania following the successive German and Soviet invasions in September 1939 of their hometown, Bialystok, Poland. In April 1941—just weeks before the genocide of the Jews began— the Melameds sailed from Japan for the United States. After the war, Leo learned that his two grandmothers, aunt, and most of his classmates from both Poland and Lithuania had perished in the Holocaust.

These two documents opened new avenues of research, and it soon became apparent that the stories of the Kovno ghetto and the unlikely Japanese rescuer were distinct chapters in Holocaust history. The focus of the Sugihara story shifted and broadened to the refugees themselves and their incredible flight across the vast Eurasian continent and beyond. There was much more to the visa story than was previously thought. Jan Zwartendijk, the Dutch acting consul, played a vital role in providing visas to enable the refugees to leave Lithuania. It was also learned that a network of Dutch diplomats provided assistance along the way, starting with L. P. J. de Decker in Latvia, A. M. de Jong in Sweden, and Nicolaas de Voogd in Japan. Equally important to the escape and safety of the more than 2,000 refugees were the untiring activities of many Jewish organizations and individuals, especially Zorach Warhaftig of the Jewish Agency and Moses Beckelman of the American Jewish Joint Distribution Committee.

The "Sugihara list" and the Melamed passport were the first two of hundreds of artifacts and photographs that were eventually loaned or donated to the Museum for the *Flight and Rescue* exhibition by individuals and institutions in 13 countries. What began as a modest linear display became a 5,400-square-foot exhibition on a piece of Holocaust history that extended far beyond the city limits of Kovno.

Objects for display are the essence of any exhibition, but much more was needed. Many individuals provided valuable research, guidance, and financial support, and the Museum expresses its deep appreciation to every person and institution whose assistance made this exhibition and publication possible. Our very special gratitude is expressed to the survivors, eyewitnesses, and their families who worked with us to make, for a brief moment, the staggering proportions so real.

Flight and Rescue is dedicated to the memory of Jeshajahu "Shaike" Weinberg, who died on January 1, 2000, just a few months before the exhibition opened.

SARA J. BLOOMFIELD
*Director, United States
Holocaust Memorial Museum*

CREDITS

Russian State Archive of Documentary
   Film and Photographs, Krasnogorsk

United Kingdom
House of Lords Record Office, London
David King Collection, London
Polish Institute and Sikorski Museum,
   London

United States
American Jewish Joint Distribution
   Committee, New York
AP/Wide World Photos, New York
Julien Bryan Collection, New York
Corbis/Bettmann, New York
Hoover Institution Archives and Library,
   Stanford University, Stanford
Leo Baeck Institute, New York
Libraries of the Claremont Colleges,
   California
Library of Congress, Washington, D.C.
National Archives and Records
   Administration, Washington, D.C.
National Geographic Society, Washington,
   D.C.
Orthodox Jewish Archives of Agudath Israel
   of America, New York
Pilsudski Institute of America, New York
Museum of History and Industry, Seattle
The Wolfsonian—Florida International
   University, Miami Beach
Yeshiva University Archives, New York
YIVO Institute for Jewish Research,
   New York

Anonymous
Mary Wayman Bakalinski
David L. Bloch
Irene Borevitz and Tamara Rozanski
Lucille (Szepsenwol) Camhi
Mrs. Zofia Dymant
Rabbi Jacob Ederman
Yonia Fain
Dr. Mark Fishaut
Joseph Fiszman
Rachele Noto Fiszman
Chana Frydman
Benjamin Gelbfish
Wanda M. Glass

Morton Goldberg
Stefan Golston
Ralph and Yvonne Harpuder
Ernest G. Heppner
Rhonda S. Honigberg
David Kirszencwejg
David Kranzler
Sarah Landesman
Masha Leon
The Family of Rabbi David and
   Zipporah Lifshitz
Günter (Gary) Matzdorff
Leo Melamed
Family of Hersh Milner
Markus Nowogrodzki
Leon Pommers
Irene Rothenberg
Richard Salomon
Edith Salton
Alexander M. Schenker
Ruth Berkowicz Segal
Dr. Norbert I. Swislocki
Henry Taca
Keiko Triguboff
Hanni L. Vogelweid
Ruth Lowenstein Wetter
The Family of Abraham Zalcgendler
Rabbi Moshe Zupnik
The Zwartendijk Family

HISTORICAL ADVISERS

Solon Beinfeld
David Goodman
David Kranzler
Alan Kraut
Hillel Levine
Michael McQueen
Pamela Rotner Sakamoto

EXHIBITION RESEARCH AND DEVELOPMENT

Gregory Naranjo, exhibition developer
Susan Blecher, registrar
Faina Balakhovskaya
Elizabeth Kessin Berman
Linda Bixby

Andrew Campana
Peggy Frankston
Pan Guang
Jerzy Halberztadt
Tina Lunson
Genya Markon
Michael McQueen
Loreta Mizariene
Carl Modig
Klaus Mueller
Jacek Nowakowski
Beth Rubin
Pamela Rotner Sakamoto
Nava Schreiber
Alina Skibinska
Kelly Smith
Xu Xin

EXHIBITION DESIGN AND PRODUCTION

Lauriston Marshall, director,
    exhibition design and production
Nancy Gillette, exhibition coordinator
Ed Alton Creative, Silver Spring, Md.
Jamie Pflieger Graphic Design,
    Washington, D.C.
Nash Brookes Associates, Rockville, Md.

Richard Ernst, production manager
Proto-Productions, Addison, Ill.
AEC Services, Inc., Gaithersburg, Md.
Atelier Architects, Washington, D.C.
Bessant Studio, Washington, D.C.
David Bobeck, lighting design
David Ferraro
Lindsay Harris
William Trossen

Jane Klinger, chief conservator
Cleveland Art Conservation, Laurel, Md.
Quarto Conservation of Books & Papers,
    Inc., Silver Spring, Md.
Eileen Blankenbaker
Brenda Bernier
Bruce Day
Lizou Fenyvesi
Alison Olson
Gail Singer
Laura Vetter

Animated Graphics and Audio-Visual
    Productions
Animation Café, Plymouth, Mass.
Firstlight Pictures, Maplewood, N.J.
Polly Petit, film research coordinator
Zoe Berman
Corrinne Collette
Raye Farr
Hiroko Kiriishi
David Stolte, audio-visual and sound

TRANSLATORS

Corporate Language Services, New York
Dina Danon
Andrew Eitavicius
Wei Feng
Nathan Gutwerk
Ed Hurwitz
Mayla Korn
Tina Lunson
Bill Mazer
Hiroko Miyairi
Abe Muhlbaum
Lydia Reese
Flora Singer
David Sitrin
Meira Zedek

*In addition, the Museum would like to thank the
following individuals for their research assistance
and advice:*

Guta Alpert, F. van Anrooij, Shulamith
Berger, Helen Elbaun Berglas, Abraham
Bick, Rabbi Morris Bobrowski, George
Borenstein, Ron Brenne, Meredith Bronson,
Abraham Brumberg, Sam Bryan, Millie
and Phil Campanella, Israel Chanowitz,
Thomas Chase, Rabbi Chopansky, Sarah
Cohen, Douglas Cole, David Crowe, Aaron
Daba, Elena S. Danielson, Norma Davidoff,
Galya Dawson, Jechil Dobekirer, Lyn
Downing, Victoria Edwards, Michael Engel,
Bob Erlewine, Victor Erlich, Carrie Feld,
Sello Fisch, Krysia Fisher, Ben Fishoff,
Jack Friedman, Astrid Freyeisen, Florian

Freud, Zlota Ginsburg, Wendy Glassmire, Denise Glick, Jonathan Goldstein, Moshe Goldszmid, Wolfe Gordon, Hy Gordon, Leo Greenbaum, Rebecca Gregson, Jan Tomasz Gross, Rabbi Samuel Graudenz, Hinda Gutoff, Paul Gutwirth, Leo Hanin, Shelley Helfand, Blume Sher Hellman, Ralph B. Hirsch, Edith Jaskoll, Chaim Kalmanowicz, Hadassah Kaminsky, Szolem Kaplinsky, Nehamaha Kaplinsky, Ryuichi Kaneko, Rabbi Yitzhak Kasnett, Kimberly King, Pat Kearns, Heidrun Klein, Maria Klein, Rabbi Moshe Kolodny, Rena Krasno, Zonia Krassnek, Aaron Kronenberg, Ida Kunda, Mr. Kuwata, Ruth Lax, Mike Le Tourneau, George Liebert, Yehezkiel Leitner, Nathan Lewin, Kong San Li, Yaacov Lozowick, Nancy Marchant, Rei Masuda, Seiichiro Matsunaga, Kathleen McCabe, Frank Mecklenburg, Roy Melbourne, Jack Michaelson, Bonni-Dara Michaels, Jerry Milrod, Sol Milrod, Masayuki Miyamoto, Josef Mlotek, Fruma Mohrer, Helene de Muij-Fleurke, Kazunori Nakayama, Sei Nakayama, Tokuhiro Nakajima, Kazuhisa Naito, Solomon Nayman, Rabbi Yaakov Nayman, Eric Nooter, Akiko Okatsuka, Ed Orbach, Mordecai Paldiel, Berit Pistora, Rina Harris Rainesaite, Amos Rappaport, Marcia Ristaino, Richard Salomon, Eric Saul, Berl Schor, Deborah Schluger, Fayge Schwartz, Stan Schwartz, Winfried Seibert, Ann Shulman, Frank Shulman, Michael Shulman, Amy Shuter, Alina Skibinska, Sylvia Smoller, Jenny So, Chaim Spilberg, Diane Speilman, Renata Stein, Irene Steinman, Tomio Sugaya, Yukiko Sugihara, John Taylor, Rabbi Marvin Tokayer, James Ulak, Danny Uziel, Diane Estelle Vicari, Marek Web, Rita Wenig, Joan Wren, Atsuo Yamamoto, Rabbi Tsvi Zakheim, Jim Zender

FOREWORD

Flight and Rescue commemorates a brief, shining moment of humanity and compassion in the midst of the hurricane of violence, persecution, dispossession of people, murder, and genocide that we know as the Holocaust.

Beyond celebration, the exhibition evoked three personal reflections that I submit to readers of this book.

First: As scholars such as Raul Hilberg, Christopher Browning, and Uwe Adam have shown, bureaucracy made the Holocaust possible. Murderous rage alone cannot sustain a 12-year-long process of pillage and genocidal slaughter. It was the regulation writers, the cataloguers, the train schedulers, the paper stampers—a vast labyrinth of bureaucrats—who identified, isolated, expropriated, rounded up, and dispatched Jews to their death. By similar behaviors, millions of non-Jewish victims were sentenced and swept into the net of death and destruction.

A special part of the joy of the story of *Flight and Rescue* is that *here* bureaucracy was tweaked. The forms, the regulations, the transit stipulations needed to cross international borders were manipulated by good men, who diverted these bureaucratic processes to save lives rather than use them to stamp out lives.

Second: Consider the heroic moral depth of these good people, Jan Zwartendijk and Chiune Sugihara. The Talmud says *yesh koneh olamo b'sha'ah achat*—there are some people who earn immortality/eternity in an hour's work. In this case, it was two weeks of work, issuing papers and stamps

and visas, etc., until they were forced to shut down. After the war, neither man spoke very much about what he did. When Consul Sugihara was asked why he acted this way, he simply said that he "acted according to a sense of human justice and of love for mankind."

Zwartendijk was a part-time Dutch consul, Sugihara a junior official in the Japanese civil service. For neither position was there a pre-requirement of moral greatness. Yet here is the record of the grandeur of their accomplishment. Every human being has infinite value. To save one life is like saving a whole world. Think of being a person who saved 2,000 times infinity; and that heroic lifesaving goodness is now multiplied and replicated in the children and the grandchildren of those who survived.

Finally, let us all remember that we walk a very fine line in telling this heartwarming, moving, and important story of *Flight and Rescue.* This true story would become a lie if we focus excessively on this miracle. After all, here were two saviors. Yad Vashem, the Israeli Holocaust Memorial Authority, has identified 17,433 righteous saviors who acted in the Shoah. But there were not two million saviors; that is why there are millions and millions of dead.

Yet we cannot overlook this small triumph. We need this account to give us some redeeming dignity, as citizens of civilized democratic countries that for the rest of eternity will be stained with the stain of indifference, of rejecting requested asylum, and of condemning many innocent refugees to death. We need the record of these two people to give us hope for human nature. The Holocaust record inexorably and eternally revealed that normal everyday people are capable of the greatest, most horrifying crimes; we need to know that normal everyday people are also capable of the most extraordinary kindness and goodness in upholding human dignity and life.

In fact, Zwartendijk and Sugihara saved not only more than 2,000 lives; they saved whole worlds of culture, of religion, and of life itself. The members of an entire yeshiva, the Mir Yeshiva, were able to get those visas. A whole little world of Torah, a repository of thousands of years of tradition and learning, of commandments and good deeds, was preserved to be replanted in the New World. This yeshiva became a part of the incredible renaissance of Jewish life and Jewish learning now occurring in America and throughout the world.

We cling to these little victories, but we also need to set them as the benchmark for ourselves. Would we live up to the model of these two good people? If life presented itself to us and asked us, "Break the rules, understand the emergency, take responsibility, and reach out beyond the ordinary to save," what would we do? That is why the United States Holocaust Memorial Museum was established: to be more than a repository of memory but also to be a living goad to conscience.

The Museum is deeply committed to memory. Memory is an act of love and of human greatness. Through memory we recover the life and the uniqueness of each of these people and snatch them from the very jaws of forgetfulness. Still, in the end we are motivated to expand Holocaust memory not just to preserve remembrance of the dead but because we are driven to turn that memory into a force for life.

So let us savor this little triumph and let us follow the instruction given by that great moral philosopher, Maimonides, to read the great religious narratives not simply for memory, but to be challenged by our predecessors' model. Let each of us read this story of *Flight and Rescue* and then ask: when and in what way will my actions reach those of Chiune Sugihara or Jan Zwartendijk? Who seeks asylum in our country? What refugees knock on the doors of our consulates? What superior's instruction should we resist in order to save a life or uphold human dignity—as they did? If we ask such questions of ourselves, that would be a tribute to their memory. That would be the promise of life's triumph in the future and not just in the past.

Rabbi Irving Greenberg
Chair, United States
Holocaust Memorial Council

Flight and Rescue is a story about Jewish refugees. In the late 1930s, the number of Jews fleeing Nazi persecution rose sharply as a consequence of Germany's annexation of Austria (the *Anschluss*) in March 1938, the widespread terror of *Kristallnacht* (November 9–10, 1938), and the Nazis' intensified policy of ridding Greater Germany of all Jews through emigration.[1] The plight of Jewish refugees seeking safe havens and the unwelcoming response of most nations provide the broad historical context for the exhibition *Flight and Rescue* and this publication. A relatively unknown aspect of this history concerns the Jewish response to the refugee crisis, particularly the critical help given to tens of thousands of Jews by a major organization, the American Jewish Joint Distribution Committee. The "Joint," as it was called, deployed staff abroad to work behind the scenes with governments and consulates on emigration matters and with local Jewish relief organizations around the globe, through which it channeled millions of dollars.[2]

The outbreak of World War II in the fall of 1939 and its changing course over the following two years set the stage for this story of Jewish refugees who escaped not from Germany but from Poland and neighboring Lithuania. Time and again, they were buffeted about, their choices constricted or shaped by major events of the war beyond their control. Many were members of Polish Jewry's prewar political, cultural, and religious elite, who fled from Poland to Lithuania after the war began to escape the tyranny not only of Nazi Germany but also of the Soviet Union. Between 1939 and 1941, the two powers were aligned as the result of having signed

a non-aggression pact on August 23, 1939. This agreement became the basis for dividing Poland into German and Soviet zones after Germany and then the Soviet Union invaded the country on September 1, 1939, and September 17, 1939.

During the first nine months of the German-Soviet pact's existence, the small but strategically situated Baltic States of Lithuania, Latvia, and Estonia clung to a tenuous independence and neutrality. Then, on June 15, 1940, the Soviet Union seized the Baltic States and officially annexed them on August 4, 1940, shoring up its western flank following the German invasion of western Europe. (German troops entered Paris on June 14, 1940.) The loss of Lithuania's independence heightened the fears of the Polish refugees who had hoped to wait out the war there or use the country as a base for emigration to the United States or Palestine. Knowing that the USSR denied its citizens freedom of movement, including emigration, many

OPPOSITE: Viennese Jews waiting in line at the Margarethen police station in order to obtain exit visas to leave Austria, 1939. *Österreichisches Institut für Zeitgeschichte, Bildarchiv, Vienna*

ABOVE: Jewish refugees waiting to board ship at the port of Lisbon, Portugal, to sail to the United States, 1940. The Joint helped arrange transportation. *American Jewish Joint Distribution Committee Photo Archives, New York*

and early 1941 were among the singularly fortunate few. They were part of the trickle of Jews who were able to flee to safety by unusual channels after the war began and after overcoming seemingly insurmountable barriers raised by the hostilities. These included disrupted consular activities and transport, the closing of borders by neutral powers, and—an especially high hurdle for many of the refugees in Lithuania in 1939 and 1940—the German, Soviet, and Lithuanian restrictions on the emigration of Polish citizens of military age. All emigration during this period was difficult and expensive, and in this instance as in others, the Joint came to the rescue by paying part or all of many refugees' transportation expenses.

After the fall of Denmark and Norway to the German naval and land forces in April 1940 effectively closed the Baltic Sea to air and sea transit, only one escape route was open to the refugees. Traveling eastward on the Trans-Siberian Railroad, they crossed the vast stretches of the Soviet Union to Vladivostok, then went by ship to Japan and points beyond. Reports sent to the Joint by leaders of the small Jewish community in Kobe, Japan—known by its cable address Jewcom—carefully recorded the arrival in Japan of 2,178 Polish Jews between July 1940 and June 1941. This figure represents a minuscule number of the millions of Jews trapped in Poland, Lithuania, and other occupied territories of eastern Europe once World War II began.[4]

Before the United States entered the war in December 1941, it led the world as a haven for Jewish refugees, but American doors opened more reluctantly after the outbreak of hostilities in Europe in 1939. Of the 2,178 Polish Jews who reached Japan, a total of 532 eventually sailed for the United States, but hundreds more saw their hopes to do so dashed. Although American public opinion condemned Nazi persecution, popular attitudes as well as official policies opposed large-scale immigration of Jews. Such views

Nazi police searching Jewish men for weapons in Warsaw, Poland, fall 1939. In November 1940, nearly 400,000 Jewish men, women, and children would be confined within the sealed Warsaw ghetto. *Bildarchiv Preussischer Kulturbesitz, Berlin*

refugees felt that escape had become a matter of "now or never." The exhibition includes a display of police mug shots from the archives of the former Soviet secret police in Lithuania, which attests to the refugees' fears of arrest by the Soviets— a fate endured by the young Zionist leader Menachem Begin, the future prime minister of Israel, who was imprisoned in October 1940 on charges of "conducting anti-Soviet work that is sharply hostile to the USSR."[3]

In the end, the refugees who escaped from Soviet-occupied Lithuania in late 1940 were shaped by the Great Depression, when antisemitic, xenophobic, and nativistic prejudices thrived in a time of high unemployment. After World War II began, the State Department's fear of spies entering the United States led to even more stringent policies that adversely affected the visa applications of many refugees arriving in Japan in 1941. As a consequence, the number of Jewish refugees stranded in Kobe grew, a phenomenon that occurred in western Europe on a larger scale at the port of Lisbon, Portugal.

In his ground-breaking study, *Paper Walls,* historian David Wyman describes the specific bureaucratic obstacles that hindered thousands of Jews from reaching the safety of American shores between 1938 and 1941. The Immigration Act of 1924, which its congressional sponsors described as "an act to limit the immigration of aliens into the United States," set fixed numerical quotas. Working within the framework of U.S. law and State Department policies, American consuls abroad all too often used their discretionary powers to reject applications for visas—the vitally important stamps placed in passports that permitted passage across international borders.[5] The original document of the 1924 act was borrowed for the exhibition from the National Archives and is reproduced in this publication. Also reproduced is Great Britain's white paper of 1939, on loan from the House of Lords Record Office. This statement of policy on Palestine was issued in response to the increase in Jewish immigration to the British mandate in the 1930s and established strict annual quotas intended to stem this flow.

"It is a fantastic commentary on the inhumanity of our times," wrote American journalist Dorothy Thompson in 1938, "that for thousands and thousands of people a piece of paper with a stamp on it is the difference between life and death."[6] The desperation of Jews fleeing Nazi persecution in the years 1938 to 1941 despite having failed to obtain visas was reflected in the flood of refugees who arrived in Shanghai. Many were men released from concentration camps and prisons on the condition that they leave the Reich. In just one year, between late 1938 and 1939, some 15,000 German and Austrian Jews entered this port of last resort because no visa was necessary. The response to unwanted immigrants seen worldwide was repeated in August 1939, when Japanese occupation authorities who controlled entry to Shanghai closed the door to most refugees. The city lacked suitable employment and housing for additional Europeans, and relief funds and the organizations administering them had been stretched beyond their capabilities by the arrival of so many people in such a short time.[7]

Among the last Jews to arrive in this Asian port were hundreds of Polish citizens, nearly half of the 2,178 individuals who had escaped from Lithuania to Japan. In the late summer of 1941 in preparation for the Pacific war, Japanese authorities began expelling all foreigners from the home islands. The new arrivals in Shanghai, having failed to obtain final destination visas at the American

Jewish refugees from Austria disembarking in Shanghai from the Italian ship *Conte Verde.* December 14, 1938. *National Archives and Records Administration, Washington, D.C.*

Jewish refugees seeking transit visas at the Japanese consulate in Kaunas, Lithuania, in late July and early August 1940, following the Soviet takeover of Lithuania. The blurred movement of the visa applicants vying for position in line captures well the urgency of their mission. The snapshot was taken by a member of the Sugihara household. *USHMM, courtesy of Hiroki Sugihara*

and other foreign consulates in Japan, had been issued entry permits because they had nowhere else to go. The largest, most cohesive group of Polish Jews who passed the war years in Shanghai came from one of Poland's most renowned prewar religious institutions, the Mir Yeshiva. It would be the only eastern European yeshiva to survive the Holocaust intact.

The relative safety that Shanghai provided the students and rabbis of the Mir Yeshiva and other Jewish refugees is evoked in *Flight and Rescue* by an unusual architectural fragment: a large block of brick overlaid with concrete, on three sides of which appears in relief a Menorah, the seven-branched Jewish candelabrum. This unique artifact—displayed to the public for the first time—was a decorative element from the front facade of the Beth Aharon Synagogue,

where the students and rabbis of the Mir Yeshiva assembled during the war. When the building was destroyed as part of urban-renewal efforts in the 1980s, forty years after it had fallen into disuse as a synagogue, the Shanghai Municipal Committee for the Preservation of Cultural Relics saved the fragment, which is now part of the Shanghai Museum's collections.

Saving Europe's Jews by means of immigration was no longer possible by the end of 1941. The Nazis blocked the exit of Jews from territories they directly controlled, and their anti-Jewish policy shifted radically from forced emigration to genocide. While the last few refugees from Lithuania were arriving in Japan in late June 1941, the land they had left was being transformed into a vast killing field. Following the German invasion of the USSR on June 22, 1941, in the massive Operation Barbarossa, the Nazis began implementing a plan to destroy Jewish life and culture.[8]

Flight and Rescue is set in the years 1939 to 1945. The pivotal point in the rescue story occurred in late July 1940, when Soviet officials ordered the closing of all foreign consulates in Kaunas, Lithuania. With the ending of opportunities to obtain the necessary visas for escape, many refugees desperately sought flight from immediate danger—by whatever channel possible. They had to scale the "paper walls," including the practical impossibility of doing all the paperwork necessary to obtain even the special "emergency visas" for rabbis, labor activists, and others before the U.S. consulate shut down. One refugee leader, Zorach Warhaftig, later recalled, "We had memorized atlases and the globe and had become experts in outlining to ambassadors and consuls the most intricate travel routes. Where no route existed, it was for us to create one—if only on paper, for the time being."[9] The paper route, in theory, took the refugees to the Dutch Caribbean island of Curaçao by way of Japan. In reality, the visa stamps they received did not get them beyond Japan, but once there, they were safe and could apply for visas at American and other consulates.

For a brief time, the lives of two acting consuls in Kaunas, were transformed and joined in a way that neither could have anticipated. Hundreds of Jewish refugees thronged the offices of the Dutch business-man Jan Zwartendijk, who had reluctantly agreed just a few weeks earlier to take on the part-time duties of acting consul. He signed and stamped with the official Dutch seal hundreds of declarations stating that no visa was required for entry to Curaçao and other colonies in the Dutch West Indies. With these stamps that served as destination visas, the refugees then swarmed to the gates of the Japanese consulate, where the career diplomat Chiune Sugihara also came to their rescue. Over the course of just a few frantic weeks, these two locales pro-vided efficient assembly-line operations. Zwartendijk and Sugihara issued stamps on pieces of paper that proved to be the difference between life and death.

Photographs from the Zwartendijk and Sugihara families, personal items, and the 31-page list of visa recipients (the so-called Sugihara list), borrowed from the Diplo-matic Record Office of the Japanese Foreign Ministry, evoke the role of these two res-cuers who made escape from Lithuania possible. Documenting the refugees' success in reaching Japan and the liberation from fear that Japan represented is a rich trove of photographs of them taken by avant-garde Japanese photographers who dis-played their work in a 1941 exhibition titled *Wandering Jew*.

Finally, as part of a major research effort undertaken to identify previously unknown materials, a large group of passports and other travel papers bearing the valuable Zwartendijk and Sugihara visas was ob-tained from individuals who participated in

the remarkable flight. Many of these men and women and others linked to the story welcomed us into their homes. They care-fully laid out the personal belongings and documents they had saved for 60 years, recounted the compelling details of their long, individual odysseys, and painfully shared their photographs and memories of loved ones left behind. It is earnestly hoped that this volume does justice to their story.

SUSAN BACHRACH
Curator, Flight and Rescue

TOP: Jewish refugees and local boy in Kobe, Japan, March 1941.

BOTTOM: Polish yeshiva students outside their group home in Kobe, Japan, March 1941. *Photographs by Toru Kono; Private collection, courtesy of the Osaka City Museum of Modern Art*

INTRODUCTION

1 FLIGHT

GERMAN INVASION

German forces attacked Poland on September 1, 1939. The underlying motive for the invasion was Adolf Hitler's desire for *Lebensraum*—living space—for the German people *(Volk)* in the east. In pursuit of new territory, German forces swept across the Polish border from the Baltic Sea in the north to the Slovakian border in the south, smashing Poland in a massive pincer movement. Two days later, France and Britain, Poland's military allies, declared war on Germany but failed to open a second front or undertake any military operations to alleviate the crushing pressure on Poland. Although Polish troops fought valiantly, they were woefully underprepared and no match for the better-equipped mechanized German forces. After only eight days of fighting, German soldiers laid siege to the capital city of Warsaw.

Fleeing from the rapidly advancing German troops, hundreds of thousands of refugees, Jews and non-Jews, swarmed into the eastern provinces of Poland. Among those who escaped in the early days of the invasion were Jews who had been active in public and communal life. Leaders of Jewish political parties, businessmen, lawyers, teachers, writers, journalists, and physicians feared that their prominence would make them especially vulnerable to persecution. Most of the refugees intended to wait out the storm in eastern Poland, not knowing what

the future would bring. Others turned toward the Romanian or Hungarian borders or headed for the Soviet frontier, which they hoped to cross in the event of German victory. Many responded to the Polish government's call to arms and set out for Brest, where fighting forces were said to be assembling.

Many of the refugees fled with no clear-cut destinations. Moving eastward, sometimes in blind panic, they clogged the roads, traveling on foot and on bicycles, in carts, cars, and trucks. When they needed to rest, they slept in ditches or sought refuge in empty buildings and barns. Life on the road was perilous for these defenseless columns of civilian refugees, who were subject to strafing by German aircraft.[1]

OPPOSITE: Civilians flee Warsaw following the German invasion of Poland. *Julien Bryan Collection, New York*

BELOW: Nazi dictator Adolf Hitler reviews German troops during the invasion of Poland, September 1939. *Yad Vashem Photo Archives, Jerusalem*

ABOVE: Warsaw residents
escape from their homes
as the city is set afire by
German incendiary bombs.
Corbis/Bettmann, New York

RIGHT: A residential area of
Warsaw flattened by German
bombs. *USHMM, courtesy of
Julien Bryan*

Most of the Jewish refugees, like those who intended to report for military duty, were single or married young men who left family members behind because of rumors that Jewish women and children were less likely to be mistreated. Many believed their absence would be temporary. They packed lightly, not even taking photographs of family members they would presumably see again soon.[2] Because they had fled so suddenly, few had made contingency plans or took the time to prepare adequately for the treacherous journey. Wanda Glass recalled that her husband, Marjan, had volunteered to dig trenches in an attempt to fend off the German forces' entry into Warsaw. While working, he met a taxi driver who offered to drive the family eastward in exchange for money and fuel. Marjan readily accepted the offer, stopped off briefly at his home to gather his astonished wife, mother-in-law, brother-in-law, and son, and left without taking the time to change from his soiled work clothing.[3] The Glass family ultimately made it out of Poland. Others, terrorized by the dangers of life on the run or finding separation from their families unbearable, eventually returned home.

Those who made their way back to Warsaw found the city charred and smoldering from the murderous aerial bombardment. Bombs dropped over the center of the city had rapidly ignited fires, which were at first contained but later blazed out of control, destroying entire city blocks. By the time the bombing stopped, 25 percent of Warsaw's buildings were damaged or destroyed, and an estimated 40,000 civilians were dead.[4] The Jewish quarter was virtually flattened. Contemporary sources reported that some 20,000 Jews died in the conflagration, and hundreds of bodies remained buried beneath the rubble.[5]

All Polish citizens suffered during the early stages of the German occupation of Poland. As soon as German troops entered Polish cities and towns, they unleashed a merciless campaign of terror. Violence against Jews was often random and spontaneous, perpetrated not only by German officers and soldiers but also by members of the security police who accompanied them. Beatings, robbery, and public humiliation became commonplace. Ruth Berkowicz Segal vividly recalled seeing the Germans in Warsaw round up young girls for cleaning tasks.[6] Before Susan Bluman left Warsaw, she also experienced the effects of the German occupation:

We couldn't walk, we couldn't talk. We were afraid even in our own homes. And

TOP: Ris Berkowicz with her uncle, David Berkowicz, in Vilna, 1940. *Ruth Berkowicz Segal, New Hampshire*

MIDDLE: Rucksack carried by Ris Berkowicz when she left Warsaw in October 1939. At the border, German soldiers stole the contents but let her proceed. *Ruth Berkowicz Segal, New Hampshire*

BOTTOM: Work trousers worn by Marjan Glass when he hurriedly fled Warsaw ahead of the German advance on September 7, 1939. *Wanda M. Glass, New York*

ABOVE: Rabbi David Lifszyc (left) with Torah scrolls rescued from desecration in Suwalki after the German invasion of Poland. The scrolls were taken to the synagogue of Kalvaria for safekeeping, but most of them were later destroyed during the German occupation of Lithuania. *Family of Rabbi David and Zipporah Lifshitz, New York*

RIGHT: As they were easily identifiable, Orthodox Jews were among the first targets of Nazi persecution in occupied Poland. *Bildarchiv Preussischer Kulturbesitz, Berlin*

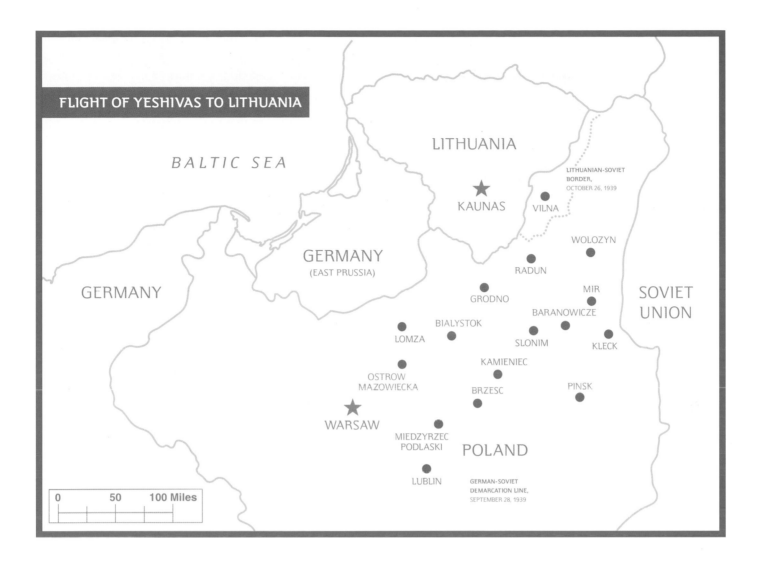

FLIGHT OF YESHIVAS TO LITHUANIA

BALTIC SEA

LITHUANIA

LITHUANIAN-SOVIET
BORDER,
OCTOBER 26, 1939

★ KAUNAS   VILNA

GERMANY
(EAST PRUSSIA)

WOLOZYN

RADUN

GERMANY

GRODNO   MIR

SOVIET
UNION

BARANOWICZE

BIALYSTOK

LOMZA   SLONIM   KLECK

KAMIENIEC

OSTROW
MAZOWIECKA   BRZESC   PINSK

★
WARSAW   MIEDZYRZEC
PODLASKI   POLAND

LUBLIN   GERMAN-SOVIET
DEMARCATION LINE,
SEPTEMBER 28, 1939

0   50   100 Miles

---

progressively the situation became worse because they picked up my father one time, they shaved off his beard, they made him work hard. We were really afraid for our father to go out. One time some Germans got into our house when my mother was by herself and beat her up.[7]

David Lifszyc, the chief rabbi of Suwalki in northeastern Poland, endured numerous indignities and threats from German authorities, including having a knife held to his throat by a Gestapo agent who demanded that the Jewish community turn over all special knives used for ritual slaughter. In Suwalki, German police had snatched Jews off the streets or taken them from their houses to build trenches and clean toilets. They purposefully took the old and weak for the harder work and beat

up young men who offered to go in their place. In late October 1939, after the German occupation forces ordered all Jews to leave the Suwalki region, Lifszyc led his family on a perilous flight through swampland to the Lithuanian border.[8]

SOVIET INVASION

The refugees who fled the German onslaught assumed they would be safe once they reached the eastern provinces. The Soviet invasion of Poland on September 17 took them by surprise. Zionist leader Zorach Warhaftig was in the

BELOW: Matzah cover, 1931, which the Lifszyc family used in observing Passover prior to fleeing Poland. *Family of Rabbi David and Zipporah Lifshitz, New York*

aid the third power in any way. The secret protocol determined the spheres of influence that would fall to each power in Poland, the Baltic States, and Finland. When the Red Army invaded Poland, Soviet leader Joseph Stalin claimed it was coming to the defense of the kindred Ukrainian and White Russian people who resided in the eastern provinces.

Polish forces, already fatally wounded by the German attack, were totally unprepared to fight a two-front war. By early October the guns fell silent and the victors divided their spoils. The area of Poland east of the Bug River went to the Soviets, who incorporated the territories into western Byelorussia and western Ukraine. The rest of Poland fell to the Reich. Germany directly annexed the westernmost areas and established a civil administration in central Poland, which they called the General Government. About 3.3 million Jews lived within Poland's prewar borders. After the partition, approximately 1.8 million of them remained in territories under German control, while some 1.5 million found themselves in Soviet-occupied Poland, including an estimated 300,000 Jews who had fled to the Soviet-held zone from the German-controlled areas.[10]

THE REFUGEES IN SOVIET POLAND

What did Poland's rapid and brutal dismemberment mean for the hundreds of thousands of Jews who had left their homes in search of sanctuary in eastern Poland? Those who managed to make it across the demarcation line into the Soviet zone, as well as locals and refugees already there, were at first assured by the Soviet presence. But soon in wide circulation was a comment that expressed their cynical acceptance of Soviet domination: "Our death sentence has been commuted to life imprisonment!"[11] Although Jews well understood that life in Soviet territory would mean material deprivation, and that prospects for emigration

TOP: German and Russian officers discuss the transfer of Brest-Litovsk to the Soviets, Brest-Litovsk, September 21, 1939. *Bildarchiv Preussischer Kulturbesitz, Berlin*

BOTTOM: Soviet soldiers examine captured Polish military supplies. *Russian State Archive of Documentary Film and Photographs, Krasnogorsk*

eastern town of Lutsk when he learned of the Soviet advance. "We could not believe our ears," he later wrote. "Never in our wildest dreams did we suppose that the Soviet Union would offer its hand in friendship to the Nazi prince of darkness."[9] What Warhaftig did not know at the time was that a secret protocol had been appended to the German-Soviet Non-Aggression Pact of August 23, 1939 (also known as the Ribbentrop-Molotov Accord, after the two foreign ministers who negotiated it). The accord stipulated that if Germany or the USSR were the object of military aggression by a third party, the other signatory would not

LEFT: Members of the Kamieniec Yeshiva study a religious text. *Family of Hersh Milner*

BELOW: Endless lines of refugees head east along Polish roads in the fall of 1939. *YIVO Institute for Jewish Research, New York*

WSTĄP DO CUKUNFTU

אײַן אין 'צוקונפט

Nakładem K. C. Żw. Młodzieży „Cukunft" w Polsce
Druk. „RENOMA", Warszawa, Karmelicka 17
Projektował H. Cyna

RIGHT: Prewar recruitment poster by artist Hersh Cyna for Tsukunft (Future), the youth group of the General Jewish Workers' League (Bund). The Bund created a network of schools, study circles, publishing houses, newspapers, summer camps, and sports clubs, and promoted the use of the Yiddish language. *YIVO Institute for Jewish Research, New York*

BELOW: Henryk Erlich (front, left) with his children Victor, Shoshke, and Alexander (standing left to right) and his wife, Sophia, and her father, Simon Dubnow, the noted Jewish historian, before the war. *YIVO Institute for Jewish Research, New York*

were extremely bleak, the general feeling was that at least their lives had been spared. Many, however, did not feel safe in their new environment.

During the early weeks of the Soviet occupation of eastern Poland, "chaos prevailed," according to Dr. K. Schwartz, a Jew and former member of the Polish Sejm (parliament), who reported at the time on conditions in Poland.[12] The Jews waited uneasily to see what would happen once the situation stabilized. The harsh realities of life under Communist domination soon blunted their early hopes. By early 1940, about 40,000 Jewish refugees, fearing arrest and persecution, had continued their flight from the Soviet zone of Poland. The remainder stayed behind, either by choice or force of circumstance.

Both native and refugee Jews suffered under Communist rule. Almost immediately after the invasion, the Soviets began a sweeping campaign to nationalize the economy, expropriating industrial plants, commercial establishments, real estate, banks, and welfare institutions. In January 1940, Soviet authorities declared that the Polish zloty would no longer be legal currency. The decree had an immediate and very drastic impact on the refugees. Until that time, they had managed to scrape by on hoarded zlotys, but now they found themselves without any means of support. Local Jews, heavily represented in the trades and industry, overnight were reduced to poverty. "With one blow," wrote Zionist leader and refugee Moshe Kleinbaum, "the entire population was placed on the same social and economic level, namely on the level of zero."[13]

Persecution of organized Jewish groups followed on the heels of the Red Army's arrival in Poland. Especially vulnerable were students and rabbis from eastern Poland's yeshivas (religious academies where Orthodox Jewish men study Judaic law, many preparing to be rabbis), which simply ceased to exist. Hundreds of students and rabbis chose not to await what the Soviets had in store for them. They knew they would have to leave Soviet territory in order to pursue their studies. Also victimized were the Zionists, who dreamed of establishing a Jewish homeland in Palestine. The Soviet authorities initially tried to win over the Zionists by assuring them they would not be persecuted in Soviet-occupied Poland and therefore should abandon plans to settle in Palestine. When the Zionist leadership proved intractable, arrests and persecution followed.

The Soviets carried out an equally ruthless campaign against members of the General Jewish Workers' League, commonly known as the Bund. Organized in response to the anti-Jewish pogroms in tsarist Russia, the Bund had reached political maturity in interwar Poland. As a legal political party, the Bund fought for Jewish cultural self-determination in eastern Europe, rallying Jews to the cause through its support of trade unions and organized labor. Any illusions that the shared goal of commitment to the worker would win the Bund sympathy from the Communist occupiers were quickly dispelled in the face of mass arrests. Only days after the Red Army marched into Poland, the Soviets arrested the prominent Bundist leaders Henryk Erlich and Victor Alter. News of the arrests reverberated through the Bund's membership, scattered across Poland after the German attack. Refugee Joseph Rothenberg was heading east with a group of Bundist colleagues when he learned about the arrests. Stunned by the news, Rothenberg recalled that "great misfortune [had] happened."

ABOVE: Butterfly ornament from a wine bottle stopper that Gizela Schenker took with her as a good-luck charm when she was deported from Poland in 1940 by the Soviets. *Alexander M. Schenker, Connecticut*

BELOW: Forced laborers clear trees for the Baikal-Amur main-line railroad, Siberia, 1933. *Memorial Society Museum, Moscow*

ABOVE: Vilna before the war.
*National Geographic Society,
Washington, D.C.*

RIGHT: Synagogue in Vilna
during the 1930s. *Orthodox
Jewish Archives of Agudath
Israel of America, New York*

Friend Leybetshke came back into the city in the morning and told us that during the night, Erlich had been arrested.... The terrible news of Erlich's arrest shocked everyone."[14]

More bad news came in November 1939, when Moscow ordered all refugees residing in Soviet-occupied Poland to register for Soviet citizenship. Failure to do so, it was implied, would mean exile to Siberia. Despite the threat, many refugees chose not to register with the authorities because they knew that accepting citizenship would preclude any chance of returning home. Once the deadline had passed, for many their worst fears became a reality. Refugees such as Alexander Schenker and his mother, together with his aunt, cousin, and grandmother, were arrested and deported to the Soviet interior in June 1940. They endured primitive conditions and subzero temperatures in an unpopulated region where the winter snow did not melt until May. Barely

15 years old, Alexander was sent to a camp at Murzhe-Kudangskii, about 400 miles northeast of Moscow, where he was forced to build roads and work as a lumberjack.[15]

The prospect of permanent exile was unbearable for some refugees. Penniless and ill prepared for such a life and despairing of seeing their families in the German zone again, they headed home. As an American observer noted, "The most striking commentary on the present situation of refugees in Russian occupied Poland is the bald fact that . . . there has been a small but continuing migration of *Jewish* refugees from the cities of Russian occupied Poland to Warsaw."[16]

TO LITHUANIA

In early October 1939, rumors began to circulate, and were soon confirmed, that the Soviets planned to return to Lithuania the historic capital of Vilna and its environs. Included in the Soviet-Lithuanian territo-

FLIGHT

rial agreement was a critical provision that
permitted the Soviets to post standing
forces throughout the country. Lithuanian
leaders naturally hesitated to allow a Soviet
foothold in their territory. However, the
temptation to regain the historic capital,
combined with the realization that they had
no choice but to yield to the Soviet demand,
made their decision easier. The Soviet-
Lithuanian Mutual Assistance Treaty was
signed in the Kremlin on October 10, and a
few days later, Soviet troops were established in military bases throughout Lithuania. On October 28, the Soviets officially
transferred Vilna to Lithuania.

For the Jews under Nazi or Soviet domination in Poland, the unexpected news was
a glimmer of hope. Fondly referred to as
the "Jerusalem of Lithuania," Vilna was an
important center of Jewish learning and
culture. Now that it was restored to politically independent Lithuania, the Jews
hoped it might provide sanctuary in war-
ravaged Europe. Even a brutal October
pogrom in Vilna that left one Jew dead and
200 others wounded did not slow the steady
migration of Jewish refugees to the district.[17] About 15,000 fled to Lithuania,
mostly to Vilna and surrounding regions, of
whom about 70 percent had left homes in
the German zone.[18] Some of them hoped to
wait out the hostilities in neutral Lithuania;
others planned to use it as a temporary
haven while arranging for their escape from
Europe.

The first wave of the exodus, when thousands of refugees entered Vilna unhindered,
lasted until the Soviets secured the re-
aligned frontier between Soviet Poland and
Lithuania in November 1939. The journey
was usually uneventful, but it could be uncomfortable. The refugees who started out
during an unseasonably warm September
had packed lightly, assuming they would
soon be returning home. Chana Giterman
Frydman recalled that her mother had to
persuade her to take along a light spring

coat when she left Warsaw.[19] Many people were unprepared for the onset of cold weather. One refugee remembered stopping off at the train stations en route to Vilna, where the tanks of boiling water enabled him and his companions to make hot drinks.[20]

Most of the family groups went to Vilna as part of the first wave of the exodus, often joining husbands and fathers who had gone earlier. Leo Melamed, a child in 1939, remembered the night he and his mother received a message from his father to join him in Vilna without delay. They packed frantically. "It was imperative for my mother and me to leave Bialystok, take the train out of Bialystok to Vilna that very night, in order to be in Vilna when the transfer of government occurred, because after that we would not be able to get into Lithuania."[21]

A second wave of refugees entered Lithu-ania illegally from November 1939 until

LEFT: Masza Swislocki with her son (center) and friends in a prewar photograph that she was able to retrieve from her Warsaw home damaged by German bombing. *Dr. Norbert I. Swislocki, New York*

BELOW: The Swislocki family observes Passover in Vilna, 1940. *Dr. Norbert I. Swis-locki, New York*

David Kirszencwejg (far left) and Chaim and Perla Kirszencwejg (center), with friends from Warsaw, in Vilna, 1940. *David Kirszencwejg, New York*

January 1940, when crossing the border was often at great physical peril but still possible. Many sneaked over on New Year's Eve, counting on the guards to be drinking and celebrating rather than patrolling vigilantly. Masza Swislocki took her three-year-old son Norbert to join her husband in Vilna in November. One hand gripping a suitcase, the other holding Norbert's small hand, she set off from Warsaw, trudging through the snow. Years later, Norbert had vivid memories of the harrowing journey:

> I remember crossing snow-covered fields with my mother in the middle of the night, hiding among the trees while a patrol crossed. She would tell me to lie down in the snow and keep quiet. To protect me from the cold she would lie down in the snow and I would lie down on top of her.[22]

Traumatized by their personal experiences reaching Vilna or frightened by reports from others who had managed to cross the border, the refugees already in the city who had sent for their families lived in torment until they were safely reunited. Yiddish

stage actress Rose Shoshana Kahan arrived in Vilna in December 1939 and worked tirelessly to bring her two grown sons to the city. As she later recounted:

> Today Pinchas Schwartz told me that since he is occupied with bringing his wife and child, he constantly has images before his eyes, terrible nightmares. . . . This night he dreamt that his child is running through the snow and the soldiers are chasing the child. I remained standing, as if paralyzed, how did he dream my nightmare?[23]

Ultimately, Kahan's attempts to bring her sons to safety were in vain. Although they did manage to reach Vilna, Lithuanian police subsequently arrested them for crossing the border illegally. After January 1940, the Soviets sealed the frontier, and harsh winter weather rendered passage virtually impossible.[24]

The second wave of refugees to flee to Vilna included members of organized Jewish groups in Poland, particularly young Zionist pioneers and students and rabbis from Poland's yeshivas, who relied on the resources of their organizations to cross the border illegally. The young Zionists typically traveled on their own as far as Lida, the refugees' main point of departure from Soviet Poland, where they were met by Zionist emissaries who distributed money and food. Guides, either local farmers or professional smugglers, then led them to Ejszyszki, just inside the Lithuanian border, where they made contact with members of the movement who took them to Vilna. Approximately 1,400 of the 2,500 members of Zionist youth groups who subsequently registered in Vilna managed to sneak across the border after it was sealed.[25]

Refugees without organized groups to help them had to rely on ingenuity, bribery, or sheer luck to make it to Lithuania. Their experiences ranged from uneventful to terrifying. The only thing that was certain was the frighteningly arbitrary behavior of the border guards and soldiers. They might look the other way, particularly if bribed, but sometimes they arrested the refugees or shot at them to scare them away.[26] Those who could afford to hire guides often reached Vilna without incident. But some guides were unscrupulous, abandoning the refugees without a trace after collecting payment.

Setting out without the security of guides meant taking a calculated risk. Maks and Zofia Sztejn crossed the border on New Year's Eve 1939, successfully gambling that the guards would be too busy celebrating to intercept them.[27] Others donned peasant clothing that enabled them to cross the frontier undetected. Sarah and Hirsch Kupinsky set out with their mother to join their father and his brother after the Soviets had sealed the border. Decades later, brother and sister recalled their fears as they hid in a barn while the farmer distracted the border guards nearby who were searching for them. Emerging safely, the family borrowed farm clothing and continued on to Vilna dressed like Polish peasants.[28]

Janek Goldstein (left) and Markus Nowogrodzki in Vilna, April 1940. *Markus Nowogrodzki, New York*

The result of detection could be arrest and deportation to Siberia. Although many refugees recounted stories of arrest and subsequent release, others were less fortunate. On his first attempt to reach Vilna, Samuel Soltz and a friend took a train as far as Merchikantz, a town near the Lithuanian border, hoping to continue on to Vilna on foot. Apprehended by a Soviet patrol, they were arrested and thrown into prison. Soltz was able to convince his captors that he was actually a Russian patriot heading back to the Soviet zone from Lithuania. His friend was not so lucky: "Leshes was brought to be examined after me and I managed to tell him that I would wait at the station for him until evening. To my great sorrow, he did not arrive. Among his things they found a small topographic map and he was sent to Siberia."[29]

Despite these obstacles, the flow of refugees across the border continued. For most, the chief motive to hazard the journey was the prospect of what might happen if they stayed behind. For many others, the motive was the pursuit of a peaceful sanctuary in war-torn Europe.

2 REFUGE

PROFILE OF THE REFUGEES

The refugees who reached Lithuania were by no means typical of Poland's prewar Jewish population. The majority came from a diverse, educated elite who had the financial resources or organizational support needed to escape. Ultimately, 15,000 Polish Jews found refuge in Lithuania, 11,000 of them in Vilna. Most were adult males; of the 10,000 refugees who had registered with the local relief committee by the beginning of 1940, fewer than 2,000 were women, and barely 500 were children.[1] One relief worker in Vilna estimated that fully half of the refugees who reached Lithuania from Poland were members of organized religious or political groups that had, in some cases, been transplanted sometimes almost intact.[2]

The Zionist pioneers and yeshiva students and rabbis who went to Vilna were the most tightly organized of the groups.[3] Hundreds of young Zionist pioneers, preparing for life in Palestine, had been living on agricultural training farms in eastern Poland. Already separated from their families, they readily heeded the call from their coordinating committees to gather in Vilna. The yeshiva students' flight was more spontaneous. In normal times, the yeshivas' deans determined institutional policy, and the students were expected to follow their lead. But when the students in many of eastern Poland's yeshivas learned that Vilna was

OPPOSITE: **Crowded market in Vilna's Jewish quarter, c. 1940.** *American Jewish Joint Distribution Committee Photo Archives, New York*

ABOVE LEFT: **David, Perla, and Chaim Kirszencwejg in Vilna, 1939.** *Joseph Fiszman, Oregon*

ABOVE RIGHT: **Szymon Malowist and his daughter Irena in Vilna, 1940.** *USHMM, Gift of Irene Rothenberg*

LEFT: **Benjamin Gelbfish, a student from the Lublin Yeshiva who escaped to Vilna in 1939.** *Benjamin Gelbfish, New York*

ABOVE: Polish writers' group at a hostel in Vilna, March 1940. *Ruth Berkowicz Segal, New Hampshire*

RIGHT: Prewar press pass issued to Josef Fiszman. *Joseph Fiszman, Oregon*

BELOW RIGHT: Writer Josef Fiszman at his desk in 1940 at the Yiddish Scientific Institute (YIVO), established in Vilna in 1925 for the study of Jewish life in eastern Europe. *Joseph Fiszman, Oregon*

REDAKCJA DZIENNIKA
„Unzer Express"
w Warszawie

LEGITYMACJA   № 48
Okaziciel niniejszej legitymacji,
P. *Josef Fiszman*

jest współpracownikiem naszego pisma

Naczelny redaktor

Sekretarz

193 9

a benefit."[7] With a population of slightly less than 2.5 million, Lithuania struggled to absorb the 460,000 inhabitants of Vilna and the surrounding district. About 100,000 were Jews, 70,000 of whom lived in the city and made their living in retail trade or as industrial workers.[8]

Before being restored to Lithuania, Vilna was one of the poorest regions in Poland. The Soviets had further impoverished the district during their month-long occupation after mid-September 1939. Soviet troops systematically emptied the city's shops and storehouses. Manufactured goods and raw materials were either requisitioned or purchased with Soviet rubles that the territorial transfer rendered worthless.[9] "When evacuating Vilna," Zionist leader Moshe Kleinbaum observed, "the Russians helped themselves liberally to whatever they wanted. Radiators were removed from homes, beds and mattresses from hospitals."[10]

Vilna's transfer to Lithuania in late October 1939 ended the local use of Poland's currency, and the Lithuanian government steeply devalued the Polish zloty when it fixed the exchange rate to Lithuanian litas at five to one. Overnight, the price of bread jumped fivefold. The sudden increase in the cost of the basic commodity set off two days of rioting. Discontented residents scapegoated Jews, and a brutal anti-Jewish pogrom resulted.[11] The violence soon ended, but the economy was slower to recover. In mid-November, American diplomat Owen Norem reported to the State Department, "Long queues are still being formed outside the food supply depots, and stores and also banks."[12]

Hopes for a long-term recovery from the sudden financial upheaval soon grew dim. The Lithuanian government, impelled by fears of Polish cultural and demographic dominance in a territory that had long been under Poland's control, made it clear that the refugees were not welcome to settle permanently in Vilna.[13] Beginning in January 1940, work restrictions forbade all Polish refugees to hold jobs without first obtaining special police permits. Refugee writers and journalists were prohibited from writing for Lithuanian or foreign-language newspapers and were not permitted to own typewriters or any form of printing equipment.[14]

Few Jewish refugees secured the required police work permits and found jobs. Life in Vilna for the unemployed was a time of waiting and hoping. They spent hours reading in Vilna's libraries, playing cards, or gathering daily in the city's cafés and communal soup kitchens to discuss escape options with friends and colleagues.[15]

But there were exceptions. "A delegation of writers went to the City President and managed to obtain permission for the writers to write," refugee Rose Shoshana Kahan noted in her diary in January 1940. "This livened our friends up a little. Writing keeps them alive."[16] Fejgla Melamdowicz found a job teaching Yiddish in an elementary school, making it possible for her to rent a one-room apartment for her family and put food on the table.[17] Moritz Sondheimer, a German Jew who had immigrated to Lithuania in the early 1930s and established a successful plastics factory in the capital city of Kaunas, employed some of the refugees in 1939 and 1940 because, as his daughter Hanni recalled, "they had no money, no clothing."[18] The young Zionist pioneers also found ways to earn a little money. Samuel Soltz shared living quarters with other young Zionists, who pooled their earnings: "Because work was hard to find, we decided to buy saws and axes and to go out and cut firewood for the homes."[19]

REFUGEE RELIEF

The sudden devaluation of the zloty hit the Jewish refugees in Vilna particularly hard.

Heading the refugee relief effort in Vilna was Moses Beckelman's first overseas assignment for the New York–based American Jewish Joint Distribution Committee. Born and educated in New York, Beckelman had been active in the city's social services community throughout the 1930s. Arriving in Vilna in October 1939, he faced a refugee crisis of staggering proportions. With his colleague Yitzhak Giterman, Beckelman arranged to feed, house, and clothe thousands of people, as well as provide care for children and the elderly, sponsor cultural activities, and offer vocational training.

At the end of 1939, Beckelman and Giterman set out for Stockholm on an Estonian passenger ship. Beckelman planned to send uncensored reports to the home office in New York and then return to Vilna; Giterman hoped to flee Europe. The Germans seized the ship, and both men were arrested. Giterman was sent back to Poland, where he continued to work for the JDC. He perished during a Warsaw ghetto action in January 1943.

Beckelman was able to return to Lithuania, where he became a master negotiator in his struggles to support the refugees despite an ailing economy and a maze of Lithuanian regulations. He left Lithuania in February 1941 and was posted to South America by the Joint.

PHOTO: *American Jewish Joint Distribution Committee Photo Archives, New York*

Those who had managed to escape from Poland with zlotys in hand found themselves impoverished literally in a single day. Local relief organizations felt the pressures immediately: "The number of people who have to be supported has increased considerably. Persons who were formerly in the possession of considerable amounts of money are now compelled to ask us for support."[20]

The refugees' lifeline was the American Jewish Joint Distribution Committee (commonly called the "Joint" or the JDC)—the main avenue through which American Jews channeled aid to the Jews of Europe during World War II. The JDC's relief work in Vilna began when Polish Jew Yitzhak Giterman, the director of the Joint's activities in Warsaw, went to the city while it was still under Soviet occupation. On October 11, 1939, Moses Beckelman arrived from the United States to direct the Joint's Lithuanian operations; Giterman became his deputy.[21] Under Beckelman's leadership, the Joint worked cooperatively with local relief agencies and a handful of other foreign organizations to provide food and shelter for the desperately needy refugees from Poland.

In the nine months after war broke out, the Joint spent nearly $750,000 in Lithuania alone to support some 15,000 Jewish refugees and about 60,000 local Jews.[22] In early 1940, Samuel Schmidt observed, "Had it not been for the money made available by the Joint . . . I would have found 12,000 derelicts here instead of human beings all retaining their self respect."[23]

The Joint funded two Jewish relief organizations in Lithuania: The Ezra Aid Organization, based in Kaunas, had the primary task of supporting the Jewish refugees across Lithuania, and the Refugee Relief Committee in Vilna supported the majority of the Jewish refugees in that district. By the end of January 1940, reported Beckelman, the two organizations had provided care for more than 10,000 people.[24]

In Vilna, the Refugee Relief Committee oversaw a network of 47 dormitories and 52 communal kitchens, whose patrons, Beckelman noted, tended to gather by "professional, occupational or political affiliation."[25] Various Zionist groups, journalists, writers, and Bundists each had

AIDING JEWS OVERSEAS

CABLEGRAM

JOINTDISCO NYK.
REFUGEE SITUATION CRITICAL THOUSANDS FLEEING WAR
ZONES STOP EMERGENCY APPROPRIATION URGENTLY NE
FOR FOOD CLOTHING SHELTER MEDICAL AID CHILD C
STOP EMIGRATION ASSISTANCE VITALLY NECESSARY
JOINTFUND LISBO

Report of The American Jewish Joint Distribution Committee, Inc. for 1940 and the first 5 months of 1941

dining rooms. The Zionist pioneers, who had their own coordinating committee, and the yeshiva students, under the supervision of Vilna's Orthodox spiritual leader, Rabbi Chaim Ezer Grodzinski, naturally assembled in groups.[26]

The committee reviewed each group's budget and administered the funds largely provided by the Joint. It also maintained a central food purchasing office and warehouse and established a bakery staffed by refugees that supplied the communal kitchens.[27] At the beginning of 1940, Beckelman estimated that it cost about $8.45 to support each refugee for a month in the communal kitchens and dormitories. About half of that amount was earmarked for housing and the rest for food, heating, and modest cash relief. This communal arrangement proved far more economical than distributing funds to individuals for housing and food, which elsewhere in Lithuania cost $10.14 per person.[28] Another advantage of this arrangement was that it provided the refugees with a welcome social outlet.

Several of the better-organized groups established their own communal housing. Upon arriving in Vilna in mid-November 1939, Samuel Soltz learned from the Refugee Relief Committee that friends had set up a group home for members of the Mizrachi pioneers, a religious Zionist youth movement. He moved into their five-room apartment on Vangloba Street. "Every day," wrote Soltz, "new members, who crossed the border, joined us."[29] The apartment eventually housed 36 members of the group, resulting in a chronic shortage of beds, linens, and even shoes.[30]

Despite crippling budget shortfalls, the Joint, through its local affiliates, saw to it that none of the Jewish refugees in Lithuania went hungry or homeless. Although few new refugees arrived after January 1940, the relief rolls grew steadily.[31] At times, the rations in the dining rooms were rather meager. Moshe Kleinbaum reported that "the portion [the refugee] receives, to be sure, is enough to keep him from starving, but it is not capable of satisfying a person's hunger."[32]

OPPOSITE, LEFT: Fund-raising report of the American Jewish Joint Distribution Committee summarizing its work on behalf of Jewish refugees worldwide during 1940–1941. *National Archives and Records Administration, Washington, D.C.*

OPPOSITE, RIGHT: Yitzhak Giterman transplanted the American Jewish Joint Distribution Committee's Warsaw office to Vilna in the fall of 1939. *Chana Giterman Frydman, New York*

ABOVE: Refugees in a Zionist hostel in Vilna, 1940. *Lucille Szepsenwol Camhi, New York*

TOP: Refugees' soup kitchen funded by the Joint. *American Jewish Joint Distribution Committee Photo Archives, New York*

BOTTOM: Soup-kitchen ticket for a yeshiva student in Vilna. *Benjamin Gelbfish, New York*

Bluman recalled, "When I left Warsaw I took a knapsack and I had a pair of ski boots and I had one dress, some underwear. That's about it. I was just so sure that I was going to go back."[35] Securing adequate clothing or raw materials for the refugees in Vilna challenged all of Beckelman's organizational and creative skills. Because of Lithuania's precarious political situation, wedged as it was between Nazi and Soviet aggressors, merchants hesitated to part with stocks of raw materials or manufactured goods. Transportation shortages made it difficult to restock, and the October 1939 devaluation of the zloty only increased people's worries about Vilna's economy. Consequently, the Joint was sometimes unable to purchase the quantities of goods needed for the thousands of refugees. One merchant told Beckelman, "I would rather sell one overcoat a day for the next two months than sell a thousand overcoats tomorrow and then go out of business until I can succeed in getting new stocks."[36] Beckelman ultimately spent $10,000 to buy and ship clothing from Latvia.[37]

Whenever possible, the Refugee Relief Committee used the money from the Joint to purchase raw materials rather than finished goods. Refugees were then given jobs as tailors, milliners, and cobblers to produce clothing and shoes.[38] Offering this employment was often a stopgap measure designed to provide a handful of needy people with constructive work. However, because the government explicitly attempted to bar them from working, "so-called constructive relief," wrote Beckelman, "therefore is largely a matter of training and retraining, language courses, etc. rather than the creation of employment opportunities in Vilna itself."[39] To that end, the Refugee Relief Committee placed a small number of men and women as apprentices in privately owned workshops, and arranged for several groups of engineers and technicians to receive practical training from the Organization for

If food was scarce, companionship was easier to come by in the communal kitchens.

When Joseph Rothenberg arrived in Vilna after fleeing Warsaw, he was grateful to find "people with whom you feel bonded in heart and spirit."[33] Markus Nowogrodzki, whose father had been the general secretary of the Bund in Poland, also "found many, many friends" at the Vilna soup kitchens that the Joint funded for the Bund. Although far from home, he had the feeling of being among his own.[34]

In addition to food and housing, another urgent project for the Joint was finding warm clothing for the refugees, most of whom were woefully unprepared for Vilna's harsh winter weather. With temperatures remaining well below zero for days on end, the winter of 1939–1940 was the coldest the region had seen in a generation. Susan

Rehabilitation through Training (ORT), an international enterprise that prepared young Jews for various trades.[40]

Several other international organizations also aided the Jewish refugees in Vilna. The Palestine Commission for Jewish Refugees, headed in Lithuania by Zorach Warhaftig and a group of fellow religious Zionists, worked cooperatively with the Kaunas-based Palestine Office, under the leadership of Zvi Brik. These two agencies obtained and distributed certificates for entry to Palestine, arranged travel, and raised funds to help emigrants with their expenses. Warhaftig doubted that the Jews would find safety in Lithuania or anywhere else in Europe and worked energetically to rescue as many people as possible from occupied territories during his year in Lithuania. "Our policy from the start, therefore," he wrote, "was to concentrate exclusively on *aliyah* [immigration to Palestine], emigration, and rescue efforts."[41] Likewise, the American Hebrew Immigrant Aid Society (HIAS) and its multinational European affiliate known by the acronym HICEM (headed in Lithuania by Yeshayahu Rosovzky), while focusing on emigration, provided funds and logistical help to refugee and local Jews.

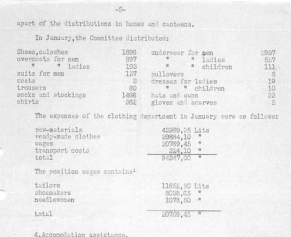

LEFT: Section of a report sent by Moses Beckelman to the Joint Distribution Committee's New York office, May 1940, itemizing expenses for clothing the refugees. *American Jewish Joint Distribution Committee Archives, New York*

BELOW: Shoemaking workshop in Vilna, established with funds provided by the Joint Distribution Committee, 1940. *American Jewish Joint Distribution Committee Photo Archives, New York*

In 1939, 33-year-old Zorach
Warhaftig and his wife, Naomi,
joined the exodus from occupied
Poland and made their way to Vilna.
Their first child, Emanuel, was born
in Lithuania in February 1940.

In Warsaw, Warhaftig had practiced
law and served as a leader of
the religious Zionists He-Halutz
ha-Mizrachi. As a refugee, he spear-
headed efforts to rescue Zionists
from occupied Poland and set up
training farms for them outside
Vilna. Together with several colleagues, Warhaftig established an
office of the Palestine Commission
for Jewish Refugees in Lithuania,
under the authority of the Jewish
Agency in Jerusalem. The Palestine
Commission's leaders worked tirelessly to send as many Jews as
possible to Palestine, establishing
escape routes, petitioning authorities, and identifying travel funds.
Before June 1940, they arranged
for 500 refugees to reach Palestine
by way of Scandinavia and France.
In late 1940 and early 1941, the
Palestine Commission helped another 700 people to exit southward
through Turkey.

In October 1940, Warhaftig and
his family left for Japan, where
he continued to help Jews trying to
leave Lithuania and others seeking
to reach Palestine from Japan.
He arrived in the United States
in June 1941. In August 1947,
he immigrated to Palestine and
later served as Israel's Minister
of Religion.

PHOTO: *Dr. Zorach Warhaftig, Israel*

Vilna's chief rabbi, Chaim Ezer Grodzinski,
turned to the Union of Orthodox Rabbis of
the United States and Canada for help in
rescuing rabbinic leaders and their students
from eastern Europe. It responded by establishing the Vaad ha-Hatzala, the Emergency
Committee for War-Torn Yeshivas (commonly referred to as the Vaad) in November 1939. The Vaad's leaders, many of them
graduates of Poland's yeshivas, believed that
the religious scholars and learned rabbis
were the spiritual future of Judaism and
merited priority in rescue efforts. Although
the propriety of giving preference to select
groups caused some disagreement within
the American Jewish community, the Joint
remained officially neutral on the topic
while acknowledging that the Vaad provided much-needed funds.[42]

REGISTRATION AND DISPERSION

On December 9, 1939, the Lithuanian
Ministry of the Interior appointed Tadas
Alekna to the newly created post of refugee
commissioner. Upon assuming his duties,

Alekna announced obligatory police registration of all refugees who, "as a result
of conditions created by war," had come
to Lithuania after September 1, 1939.[43]
The refugees greeted this news with dread.
Whether or not they complied, there were
bound to be dire consequences. Registering
would probably subject them to scrutiny
and possible expulsion, but if they evaded
the new regulation and were caught, they
were sure to be expelled. The 30 questions
on the registration form were daunting,
and the refugees worried that if they answered any of them incorrectly, they might
end up on the other side of the border.
The Refugee Relief Committee translated
the form into Yiddish and designed model
answers to certain questions. The requisite
identity photographs were also provided
free of charge to the 90 percent of the

OPPOSITE, LEFT: Registration certificate for Cypa Lifszyc. All refugees in Lithuania had to register with the Ministry of the Interior. *Family of Rabbi David and Zipporah Lifshitz, New York*

OPPOSITE, CENTER: Zlota Ginsburg, her child, and sister Yocheved in Kedainai, Lithuania, 1940. Her husband was a member of the Mir Yeshiva. *Zlota Levenstein Ginsburg, New York*

OPPOSITE, BOTTOM: Identity card for Hirsz Milner, a student at the Kamieniec Yeshiva in Poland who fled to Vilna. *Family of Hersh Milner*

LEFT: Prewar poster in Hebrew announces "organization month" for the Zionist pioneers He-Halutz ha-Mizrachi in the area of Cracow, Poland. Between the two world wars, Polish Jews were well represented in the waves of migration to *Eretz Israel,* the Land of Israel, in the British mandate of Palestine. He-Halutz promoted Zionist ideals of agricultural or manual labor and commitment to the Hebrew language and culture. *YIVO Institute for Jewish Research, New York*

applicants who could not afford to pay for them.[44]

The Refugee Relief Committee reported that the compulsory registration was part of the government's goal to diminish the Polish presence in Vilna.[45] Only those refugees who could prove they had entered the city before October 1939 would be permitted to remain. Others would be sent to provincial towns throughout the country.[46]

Most of the refugees regarded relocation as a form of banishment that would cut them

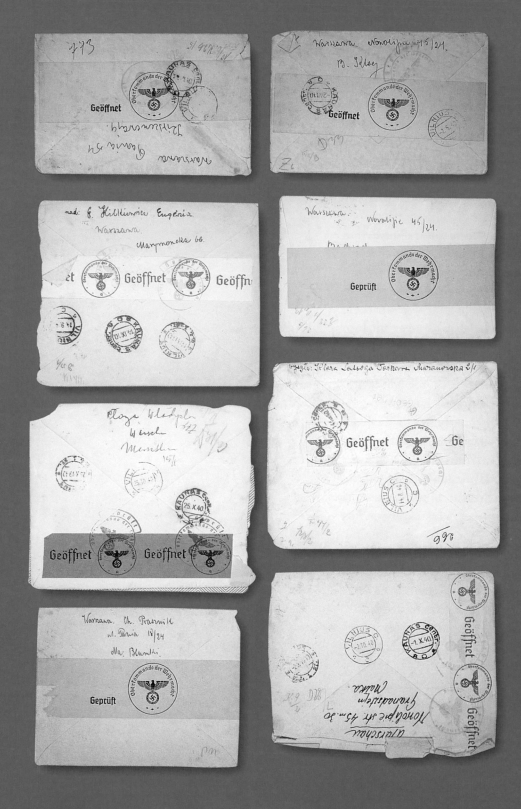

Letters from Warsaw with censor stamps. Communication with refugees was limited because the letters were opened and read by German censors.
Ruth Berkowicz Segal, New Hampshire; David Kirszencwejg, New York

THE FAMILIES LEFT BEHIND

About two-thirds of the Vilna refugees came from areas of Poland that had fallen to the Nazis. Most had left behind family and friends. Regular, if censored, news from home came in letters that took about eight days to travel from Warsaw to Vilna. The messages grew more ominous with each passing day. Joseph Rothenberg recalled that despite the censors' marks, the letters conveyed a sense of dread and impending doom.[60]

From the first days of occupation, the Germans launched a sweeping and relentless reign of terror over the Jews in Poland. Official persecution followed the random violence, totally removing all Jews from Poland's economic and social life. On October 26, 1939, Nazi authorities in the occupied area called the General Government announced that Jewish men would be subject to forced labor. A month later, all Jews in the General Government over the age of ten were ordered as of December 1 to wear "a white band, at least 10 centimeters wide, with the Star of David on the right sleeve

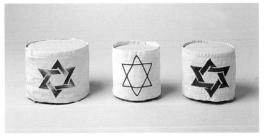

of their inner and outer clothing."[61] Jews were forbidden to travel on trains or change residence without written permission, to withdraw more than 250 zlotys (about $2.50 at the black-market rate) from their bank accounts each week, or to possess more than 2,000 zlotys in cash. A January 1940 decree required Jews to register with local authorities all property and assets, including real estate and personal belongings; these were subject to confiscation. Most of the salaried Jewish workers (business people, teachers, and clerks) lost their jobs. Stripped of assets, denied access to savings, and unable to earn wages, thousands of Jews faced starvation.

The refugees in Lithuania were not unaware of the persecution in Poland. One

ABOVE LEFT: German soldiers oversee men clearing rubble. Street roundups of Jews for forced labor were common in German-occupied Poland in 1939. Many young Jewish women had to do domestic work. *Bundesarchiv, Koblenz*

ABOVE RIGHT: Studio photograph of Sonia Nowogrodzki, which she sent from German-occupied Warsaw to her son Markus, a refugee in Vilna. She wears the required armband marking her as a Jew. *Markus Nowogrodzki, New York*

ABOVE CENTER: In late 1939 the Nazis decreed that armbands with a blue Star of David must be worn by all Jews in Warsaw and other cities within the occupied area called the General Government. *USHMM, Gift of Dina Ofman*

Brothers Lejba, David, Salomon, and Josef Berkowicz escaped to Vilna, but their families remained behind in German-occupied Poland. The wives mailed these photographs to their husbands. *Ruth Berkowicz Segal, New Hampshire*

TOP LEFT: Salomon's wife, Hanka, and their son, Julek

TOP RIGHT: Josef's wife, Genia, and their daughter, Rita

BOTTOM LEFT: Lejba's wife, Hela, and children (left to right) Henryk, Noemi, and Bernard

BOTTOM RIGHT: David's wife, Edzia, and children Alexander and Lusia

group of writers in Vilna gathered evidence of Nazi atrocities in the occupied territories and smuggled the information to the west. From Lithuania, Beckelman informed Joint headquarters in New York: "Of the Jewish population in German-occupied Poland, little need be added to what is already known. Systematic seizure of all Jewish property, exclusion of Jews from all employment or occupation, harassing and humiliating regulations including the medieval touch of the yellow badge, personal maltreatment, violence and killing of hundreds monthly continue unabated."[62]

Some of the refugees devoted their energies to finding ways to smuggle family members across the border into Vilna, but encouraging family and friends to join them presented a moral dilemma for many. The refugees who had already come to Vilna from Poland, often making the border cross-

ing at great physical peril, had sacrificed familiarity, security, and personal possessions in order to find safety. For every person who entered the country illegally, another failed. As Meri Nowogrodzki put it,

> You didn't know what's going to happen to people, so you couldn't really just say, "You must go because I know you must go." You couldn't say that. You felt that these people maybe have a better instinct. Who knew?[63]

From Warsaw, Joseph Rothenberg's sister wrote:

> When will we see one another? How often we remember you. Us and you—two worlds, no, you will never understand this. As a matter of fact, I could really be with you, too, happy, but I do not have the heart, the courage, to leave everyone behind here.[64]

TO STAY OR TO LEAVE?

The Polish Jews who reached Vilna were of two minds about whether to continue searching for havens abroad. They had strong ties to family and friends who had chosen or who felt compelled to remain in Poland. How could the refugees move even farther away when reports from occupied Poland worsened every day? For those who hoped to return home eventually, Lithuania seemed to be a safe place to wait out the hostilities. Others insisted that the safety lay only in emigration.[65] In early 1940, Beckelman wrote, "Above all is the great uncertain factor ever-present in everyone's mind—how long will Lithuania continue to hold Vilna?"[66] But as Joseph Rothenberg noted,

> We never felt, there in that little oasis Lithuania, complete security and calmness. The Soviet bases in and around Vilna constantly reminded us that today is today, but tomorrow can be something else.[67]

According to Lucille Szepsenwol Camhi, who went to Vilna with her sister, Fejga, life there was a time of "surviving and waiting." As she recalled, "Our whole existence while we were in Vilna was trying to get out, trying to get somewhere."[68] But the prospects for escape seemed to become ever more limited. "Opportunities for emigration are virtually nil," wrote Moshe Kleinbaum, who struggled to find passage for himself and his family. "Even if we ignore the lack of countries that can receive immigrants, there is virtually no traffic out of Lithuania."[69] With much of central Europe under Hitler's or Stalin's control, the only route out was via Latvia, Sweden, the Netherlands, Belgium, and France. But Germany and the USSR prohibited the Riga–Stockholm airline from carrying Polish men of military age, fearing that they might join the Allied forces abroad.[70] Germany also pressured Lithuania not to let would-be soldiers leave the country. Moshe Kleinbaum managed to secure certificates for entry to Palestine for himself

and his family, but escape from Lithuania proved to be harrowing because he was a male Polish citizen subject to travel restrictions. "My wife, daughter, and I," he recalled, "were pulled off the train on the Lithuanian-Latvian border in the middle of the night in 42-degree cold." After several weeks of frantic inquiry, he was able to obtain a Lithuanian *sauf conduit,* or "safe conduct pass." This identity paper did not classify him as a Polish citizen but instead labeled him stateless, thereby enabling him to escape. He and his family eventually made their way to Palestine via a circuitous route that took them to Riga, Stockholm, Copenhagen, Amsterdam, Brussels, Paris, and Geneva.[71]

With options so few and the risks of escape so great, some of the refugees opted for an indefinite stay in Lithuania and attempted to restore a daily routine to their lives. When Joseph Rothenberg arrived in Vilna after an arduous trek from Warsaw, he "felt like someone who had awakened from a dark, desolate nightmare in a sunny room. He touches his head, he rubs his eyes and looks around him. That is how I looked around. Was this really reality? Smiling, were these transient people actually at ease and comfortable?"[72] Life for the transplanted refugees in Vilna did offer some

Abraham and Masza Swislocki in Vilna, c. 1939. *Dr. Norbert I. Swislocki, New York*

promise of stability. Meri Nowogrodzki recalled that "people lived more or less a normal life. They had their lectures, they had their movies. And they got together, you know, and so forth."[73] Leo Melamed, a child of seven when he arrived in Lithuania, recollected the relative calm of Vilna after the unexpected flight from home: "More or less life picked up again, kind of normal," he remembered, quickly adding, however, that "it wasn't really normal. There was a constant fear hanging in the air." Like other refugee children, young Lejb Melamdowicz (as Melamed was then named) was enrolled in a Lithuanian school, quickly adapting to a new language and making friends.[74]

For many of the refugees, an active cultural life was as essential to their spiritual survival as was food to their physical existence. Rose Shoshana Kahan observed,

> In Vilna I was reborn. Again I found myself in my own house, where I found a lot of close acquaintances. A fine literary home was organized, where the refugee literary figures lived. . . . A good kitchen was created, where everyone met every day.[75]

On March 3, 1940, for the first time in seven months, actress Kahan took to the stage, performing in a play in Kaunas that was, for her, a cause for celebration.[76] Literary efforts also provided a creative outlet for many refugees. Joseph Rothenberg noted with pride that the Bundists were able to publish several books in Vilna:

> In our situation at the time it was an occurrence of the first order. . . . It was a symbol, a sign of a new beginning . . . a continuation of creative life. The Jewish libraries in Warsaw and other cities had been burned down, but the Jewish book lives on.[77]

The event was no less moving for an outside observer. Samuel Schmidt was astonished to find books published by the recently arrived refugees, which he described to his wife as "additional evidence of the indestructibility of the Jewish spirit."[78]

Compared with the sufferings of Jews in occupied Poland, where communal and economic life had swiftly and inexorably ground to a halt and brutal acts of persecution were daily occurrences, life in Vilna seemed productive and almost peaceful. "It was calm, I think rather ordinary," recalled Norbert Swislocki.[79] For a fleeting moment in 1939 and 1940, neutral Lithuania seemed a safe harbor in a storm. But the Soviet occupation of the country in June 1940 shattered the hope that Lithuania could ever be more than a temporary refuge.

OPPOSITE, TOP: Some Jewish refugee children attended school in Vilna, among them Masza Bernsztejn (far right, crouching) and Rochke Stoler (behind her, in white dress), whose parents were Bundists. *Masha Leon, New York*

OPPOSITE, BOTTOM: Report card for 1939–1940 for Lejb Melamdowicz, who is shown (first child, lower left) at his birthday celebration in Vilna, March 20, 1940. *Leo Melamed, Illinois*

BELOW: Sophie Dubnow-Erlich, a journalist for the Yiddish-language press in Warsaw before the war, speaks at a meeting of Bundists in Vilna, 1940. Her husband, Bundist leader Henryk Erlich, was arrested in 1939 by Soviet police in eastern Poland. *YIVO Institute for Jewish Research, New York*

With Molotov's concurrence, Justas Paleckis, a journalist and veteran Communist, was installed as premier and acting president. To create a new Lithuanian parliament, the Soviets called elections for July 14, the outcome of which was a foregone conclusion: Lithuania's voters faced a single list of Communist party candidates, handpicked by Moscow. Two weeks later, the new legislative body voted for formal annexation to the USSR. On August 4, 1940, Lithuania ceased to exist as an independent state and became the Lithuanian Soviet Socialist Republic.[2]

NATIONALIZATION

Even before formal annexation, Lithuanians and refugees alike felt the impact of the Soviet regime. From Kaunas, the American consul, Owen Norem, cabled Washington:

> During interim period while awaiting word of acceptance into the U.S.S.R.

expected August 1st, the Sovietization process is being intensified. . . . Yesterday all jewelry stores were relieved of their valuable gold and silver stocks and precious stones. Estate owners, former leaders and wealthy people are receiving attention.[3]

On July 26, Lithuania's new parliament nationalized all industrial and craft enterprises with more than ten workers, froze bank deposits, and transferred privately owned land to the state. The nationalization of all private buildings and all private enterprises with an annual income of more than 150,000 litas (about $25,000) followed on September 27.[4]

Hanni Sondheimer Vogelweid recalled that her family, on vacation when Soviet troops marched into Kaunas, returned to find that occupation authorities had confiscated the family's business. When Hanni's father, Moritz, went to retrieve his personal belongings from the factory, authorities turned him away. But Sondheimer was relatively fortunate: He was permitted to return as a worker in what had been his own factory, enabling him to support his family. Meanwhile, his wife, Setty, tried to withdraw their savings from the bank only to learn that all accounts had been frozen. As a further humiliation, the Soviets billeted two soldiers in the Sondheimers' apartment. Although the family was permitted to remain, they lived in fear that their activities were under scrutiny.[5]

The Soviet nationalization campaign affected Lithuania's Jews disproportionately, since most of the country's approximately 300,000 Jews lived in cities and were heavily represented in business and industry.[6] Jews owned 83 percent of the enterprises taken over by the Soviets.[7] In Vilna alone, 265 of the 370 nationalized businesses belonged to Jews, including 102 factories and workshops. Many small businesses spared the nationalization went bankrupt because new tax laws gave unfair advantage to state-run enterprises.[8]

FATE OF THE REFUGEE COMMITTEES

Even with some resources and reserves, Lithuanian Jews still had to struggle to make ends meet. What of the refugee Polish Jews, most of whom had no jobs, no savings, and no relatives in Lithuania? Rose Shoshana Kahan confided to her diary about material privations resulting from the Soviet presence: "It is the eve before Rosh Hashana [the Jewish New Year]. Again a bitter Rosh Hashana. . . . Could obtain nothing to buy. The need is terribly great."[9] Faced with empty pocketbooks and empty shelves, the refugees once again turned to the Joint and other Jewish agencies for help. There was some doubt, however, that such assistance could continue under the new regime. In August 1940, Bernard Gufler of the U.S. legation in Kaunas observed, "It is not believed that the powers now actually ruling here are likely long to tolerate relief activities with the implication that foreign charity is needed in the Soviet Republic."[10] Inexplicably, the Soviets permitted the Joint, under Moses Beckelman's continuing guidance, to go on with its relief work.[11]

Clothing supply center for refugees, funded by the Joint Distribution Committee, Vilna. *American Jewish Joint Distribution Committee Photo Archives, New York*

ABOVE: Moses Beckelman, the American social worker who directed Jewish refugee relief efforts in Lithuania. *American Jewish Joint Distribution Committee Photo Archives, New York*

OPPOSITE, TOP: Mug shot of Morduch Bernsztejn taken by the NKVD, the Soviet secret police. *Extraordinary Archive of Lithuania, Vilnius*

OPPOSITE, BOTTOM: Morduch Bernsztejn with his wife, Zelda, and daughter, Masza, spring 1940, several months before his arrest. Bernsztejn was technical secretary of the Central Committee of the Polish Bund. *Masha Leon, New York*

Challenges to the Joint's efforts came from other quarters. After the Soviet occupation, the U.S. Treasury Department prevented the transfer of American funds to Soviet Lithuania because the United States government did not recognize the incorporation of Lithuania into the USSR. The resourceful Beckelman, however, guaranteed the uninterrupted flow of funds through an arrangement with the Lithuanian Red Cross, promising JDC reimbursements at a later date. Between June and October 1940, the Red Cross made about $75,000 available to the Joint under the terms of this agreement.[12] The Vaad ha-Hatzala continued to support yeshiva students and rabbis in Lithuania by borrowing money from local Jews who were emigrating.

The Joint's effectiveness was all the more remarkable in view of the Soviets' July 1940 announcement that all Jewish institutions were to be abolished. Zorach Warhaftig officially closed the offices of the Palestine Commission and conducted business surreptitiously in the street and public gardens. The Hebrew Immigrant Aid Society ceased operations altogether.

SOVIET OPPRESSION

The continuing relief efforts in the face of these obstacles gave the refugees much needed assurances. The prospect of a full stomach offered some comfort, but it did little to quell fears of Soviet oppression. "After the occupation of Lithuania by the Soviet troops," reported a Joint memo, "the danger arose that the new authorities would treat the refugees in Lithuania in the same manner as they did in Russian occupied Poland."[13] As Warhaftig and his colleague Eliezer Szczupakiewicz wrote,

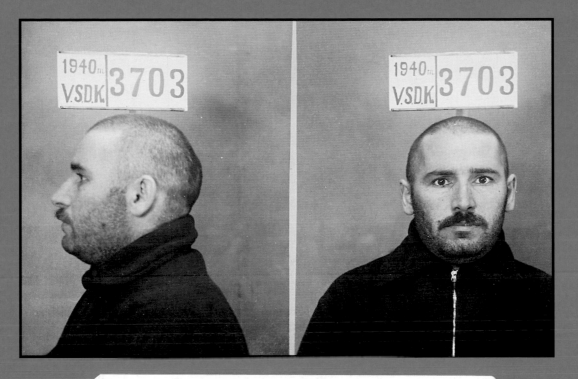

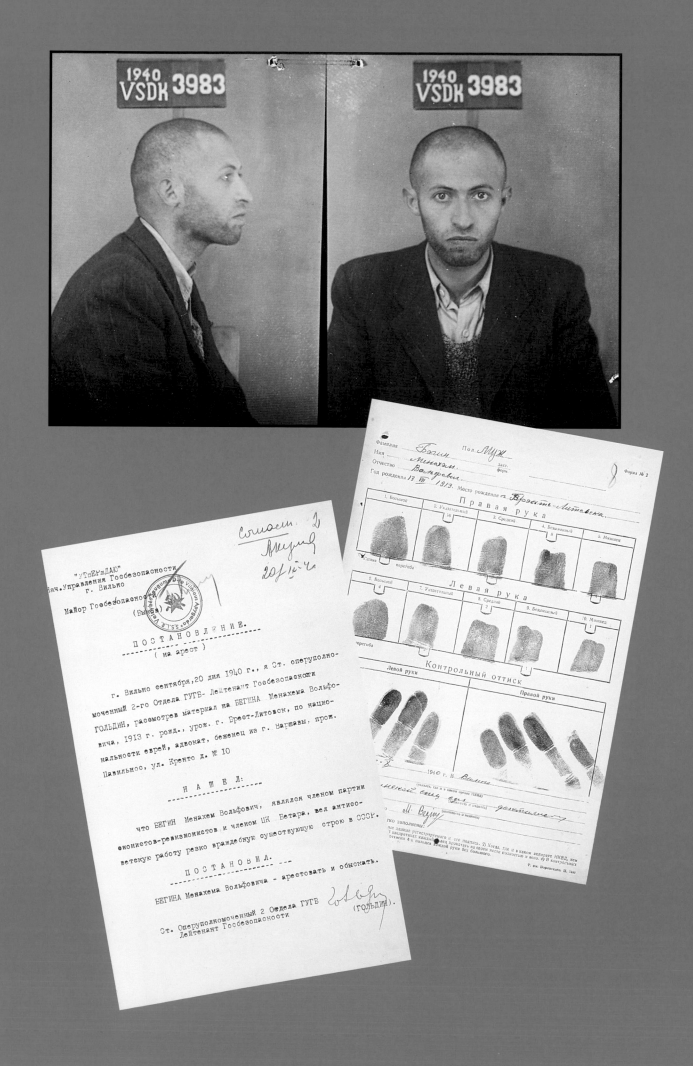

"It is impossible to describe the despair and fear of the refugees . . . especially as many refugees in [Vilna] received news from their relatives in far Siberian provinces informing them that they are frozen and starving there, even those from the deported that have money could obtain nothing for it. They prefer death to such a life."[14]

As was feared, the Soviet takeover of Lithu-ania gave rise to a relentless campaign of oppression against "anti-Soviet elements," much as had occurred in Poland. Large-scale arrests were made on the nights of July 11–12 and July 18–19, 1940. Similar actions were carried out in Latvia and Estonia. "Arrests are being made consis-tently and silently," Consul Norem reported, "usually under cover of night, and a veritable pall has descended over the country."[15] Countless Jews had fled

the German and Soviet zones of Poland because their past political activities made them targets for persecution. Now, in Soviet Lithuania, they once again found themselves at risk.

OPPOSITE: Menachem Begin was arrested after being accused of conducting "anti-Soviet work that is sharply hostile to the U.S.S.R." *Extraordinary Archive of Lithuania, Vilnius*

ABOVE: Refugee members of Betar in Vilna. Menachem Begin (front, left) headed this youth branch of the ultranationalist revisionist Zionists. *Lucille Szepsenwol Camhi, New York*

LEFT: Medallion of Betar. *Lucille Szepsenwol Camhi, New York*

Zionists, in the Soviet view, were agents of "British imperialism."[16] Accordingly, authorities suppressed all manifestations of Zionist nationalist thought. The September–October 1940 issue of the *Contemporary Jewish Record* reported, "In accordance with general Soviet policy, all expressions of distinctive Jewish nationalism were proscribed under the new regime. Zionist organizations were dissolved on July 11."[17] Some Zionist groups immediately went underground, while others scattered their membership into smaller, less visible "cells." When the Red Army marched into Lithuania, Samuel Soltz wrote, "Our kibbutz in Poniviez got instructions from the central in Kovno [Kaunas] to divide up what equipment we had among the members and to form new groups of four to five and prepare to go underground."[18]

The Zionist youth group Betar, led in Vilna by Menachem Begin (Israel's future leader), continued to meet clandestinely to discuss

world affairs.[19] Soviet agents arrested Begin in the autumn of 1940. Held in the Vilna headquarters of the NKVD (the Soviet secret police, later known as the KGB), Begin was deprived of food, water, and sleep for 60 hours, while his captors unsuccessfully attempted to wrest from him a confession of anti-Soviet activity. He was then held in the Lukishki Prison until the following spring, when he learned his fate. For the crime of participating in Zionist activities in Poland, he was sentenced, without trial, to eight years of hard labor in Siberia.[20]

Members of the Bund were vulnerable to Soviet persecution because they opposed the centralized authority of Soviet Communism. Whereas the September 1939 arrest of Henryk Erlich and Victor Alter had been a "strike at the head in order to decapitate a movement," roundups in Soviet Lithuania targeted the Bund's lower echelons.[21] Some managed to evade arrest by going underground; Icchok Melamdowicz, for example,

Deportation of people from the Baltic States to Soviet labor camps in Siberia and elsewhere, c. 1941. *National Archives and Records Administration, Washington, D.C.*

joined a band of Bundist partisans outside of Kaunas.[22]

The refugee yeshivas initially responded to the Soviet presence as the Bundists and the Zionists had done. Ordered to disband, they divided into smaller groups and went about their business clandestinely. The Mir Yeshiva dispersed its students from Kedainai to the villages of Karkinova, Shat, Ramigola, and Krak, where they continued their studies. Rabbi Eliezer Finkel, the yeshiva's spiritual leader, went to Gringishok and visited the other towns in turn. Although out of imminent danger, he realized that

if the fate of the religious Jews in Soviet Poland was any indication of what lay in store for Lithuania's refugee yeshiva students, the only road to safety lay in emigration.

When the Soviets occupied Lithuania, refugee Samuel Soltz wrote, "The refugees . . . felt that their way to the free world was now closed. All those who had escaped from Poland, like us, were now caught in the Russian trap."[23] Fearing life under the Communists, the refugees redoubled their efforts to flee despite seemingly insurmountable obstacles.

Bund leaders Victor Alter (left) and Henryk Erlich (center right, with beard) march in a prewar May Day parade in Warsaw. Also seen is Emanuel Nowogrodzki (far right). *YIVO Institute for Jewish Research, New York*

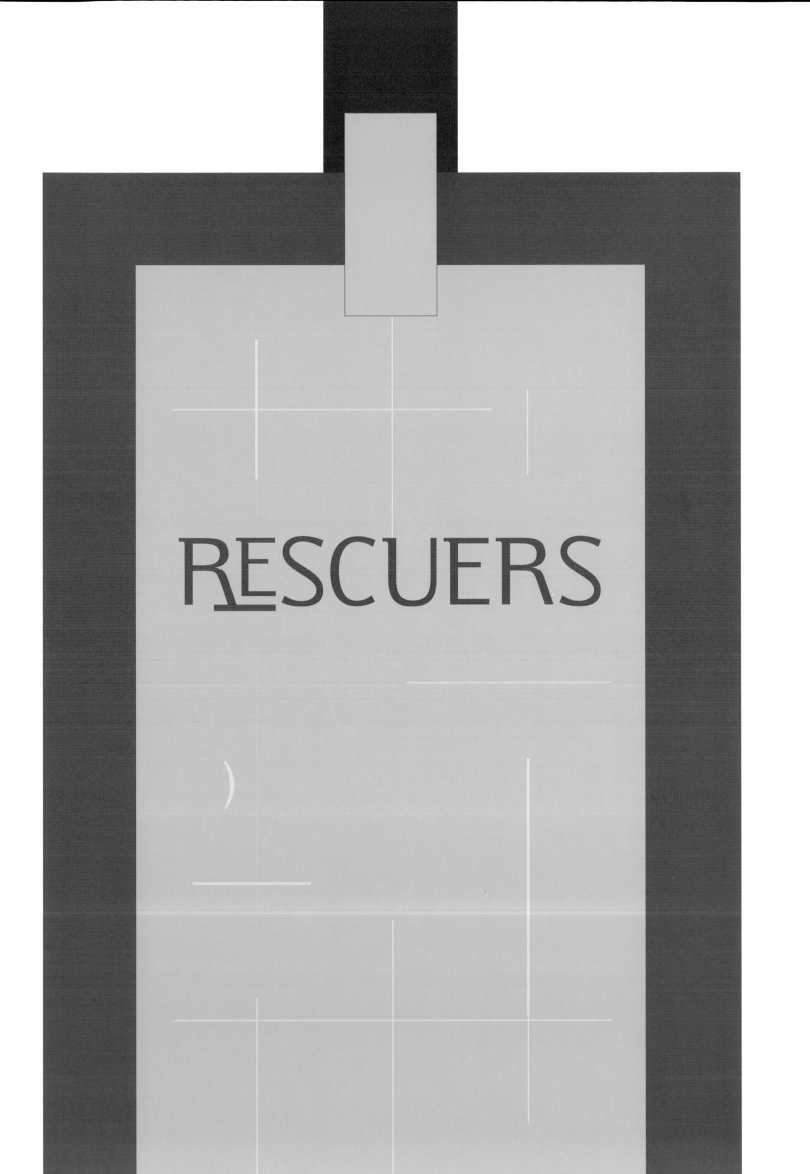

RESCUERS

Jaca Hersz-Persich

September, 1941, to
Shanghai.

TRANSIT. VISA.

Seen for the journey
through Japan (to Suranam,
Curaçao and other Nether-
la

C

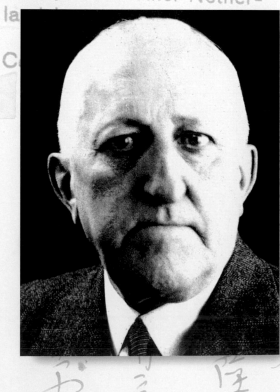

CONSULAT DU JAPON
KAUNAS. LITHUANIE

4 RESCUERS

A RENEWED SEARCH FOR HAVENS

Until spring 1940, it was still possible, though difficult, to leave Lithuania. The best escape route went west through Sweden, Denmark, the Netherlands, Belgium, and France, then south to the Mediterranean Sea and either to Palestine or the United States. Germany's defeat of Denmark and Norway in April 1940 and its rapid conquest of the Netherlands, Belgium, and, by June 1940, France effectively shut off all routes west. Escape southward became difficult after Italy, Germany's Axis partner, declared war in June and invaded southern France.

Faced with this constriction of choices, Zorach Warhaftig spent hours bent over maps, trying to work out escape routes to Palestine. "We had memorized atlases and the globe and had become experts in outlining to ambassadors and consuls the most intricate travel routes," he later recounted.[1] By the time the Soviets seized Lithuania, only two routes remained possible: south through Turkey toward Palestine or east through the Soviet Union.

The refugees who hoped to flee by the available routes faced a major hurdle: securing legal permission to travel through foreign countries. International travel often required a visa—a diplomatic notation that indicated permission to enter and travel within or across a foreign country—obtainable only from an official representative of each nation along the travel route. As an independent nation, Lithuania had hosted an international diplomatic community in the capital city of Kaunas from whom visas could be obtained. But with its incorporation into the Soviet Union came the announcement that all foreign consulates in the Baltic States must close by August 25 (later extended to September 4), as all diplomatic activities with the USSR would be centralized in Moscow.

Because of the imminent departure of the foreign legations from Kaunas, time was running out to secure the required visas, without which escape would be almost impossible. Traveling to Moscow was a risky alternative. As a general rule, the Soviet government restricted the movement of people within its territories, and it specifically forbade returning to Lithuania if the attempt to obtain a visa in Moscow failed. As a cable from the American Embassy in Moscow explained, it would be "extremely hazardous for an alien to come to Moscow expecting to obtain an American visa who after examination at the Embassy may be found to be ineligible to receive such visa and thereupon . . . is subject to exile to some Central Asian or other remote region."[2]

OPPOSITE: Clockwise from top: Jan Zwartendijk, A. M. de Jong, Chiune Sugihara, L. P. J. de Decker. The four men provided visas that made escape from Lithuania possible for hundreds of Jewish refugees.

Visa document: *Henry Taca, Florida*

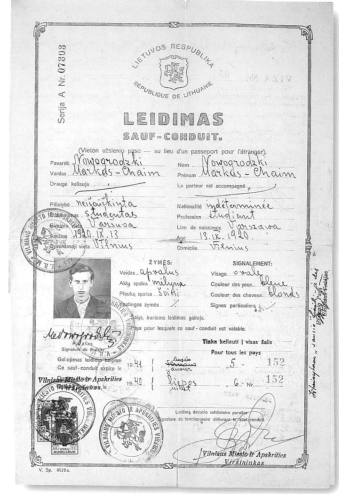

ABOVE LEFT: **Certificate of Polish citizenship for Samuel Soltz from Bialystok, Poland, issued in lieu of a passport.** *Mrs. Shmuel Soltz, Israel*

ABOVE RIGHT: **"Safe conduct" document for Markus Nowogrodzki.** *Markus Nowogrodzki, New York*

OPPOSITE: *Shanghai Evening Post*, February 4, 1941. *USHMM, courtesy of Eric Goldstaub*

To apply for a visa, each refugee needed to have a government-issued identity document, normally a passport. Many refugees, however, had arrived in Lithuania without passports, either because they had never before traveled internationally or they had left their passports behind in the rush to leave Poland. Consequently, they sought to secure documents identifying them as Polish citizens from the attaché representing the Polish government-in-exile, who worked at the British legation in Kaunas. Soviet and German proscriptions on travel by Polish males between the ages of 19 and 50 rendered Polish passports or identity papers for these men useless. Their only alternative was a *sauf conduit,* or "safe conduct pass," issued by Lithuanian authorities, identifying the bearer as "stateless," lacking citizenship of any nation. *Sauf conduits* were

prohibitively expensive—300 litas, more than $60 at the official exchange rate—and the refugees scrambled to raise the money privately or turned to the relief organizations for help.[3]

Even with identity papers in order, the question remained: who would take the refugees? The preferred destinations were Palestine and the United States, but restrictive laws and policies limited the number of Jews who could go to these places. Great Britain's Balfour Declaration of 1917 had promised the establishment of a Jewish national home in Palestine, then under British mandate. But Zionist hopes were dampened by a British white paper of May 1939 that limited Jewish immigration to Palestine over the subsequent five years to a maximum of 10,000 per year. Certificates

68TH CONGRESS
1ST SESSION

H. R. 7995

AN ACT

To limit the immigration of aliens into the United States, and for other purposes.

1   *Be it enacted by the Senate and House of Representa-*
2   *tives of the United States of America in Congress assembled,*
3   That this Act may be cited as the "Immigration Act of
4   1924."

5   IMMIGRATION CERTIFICATES.

6   SEC. 2. (a) A consular officer upon the application of
7   any immigrant (as defined in section 3) shall (under the
8   conditions hereinafter prescribed and subject to the limita-
9   tions prescribed in this Act or regulations made thereunder as
10   to the number of immigration certificates which may be
11   issued by such officer) issue to such immigrant an immigra-

U.S. Act of Congress, passed in 1924, imposed numerical quotas for immigrants. The law was still in effect in 1940. *National Archives and Records Administration, Washington, D.C.*

for entry to Palestine were distributed by the Jewish Agency in Jerusalem to Britain's representatives abroad.

Thomas Preston, the British consul to Lithuania, routinely refused to issue allocated certificates until the applicants could prove they had the necessary transit visas to reach Palestine and therefore could use the entry permits before they expired. Following the Soviets' order to close the con-

sulates, Preston unexpectedly began to issue certificates liberally on the eve of his departure. From September 1 to September 4, when the consulate closed, Preston's staff released 700 to 800 Palestine certificates to Zionist youth, rabbis, and other designated refugees.[4] In Lithuania and elsewhere in Europe, however, available certificates fell far short of demand.

Prospects for immigration to the United States were also bleak. The Immigration Act of 1924 restricted entry by means of quotas. The law made no special allowances for war victims, and the United States had no express refugee policy at the time. Thus the refugees had to contend with strict quotas apportioned on the basis of national citizenship. In 1940, there was a two-year wait for the 6,524 visas permitted annually under the Polish quota.[5] Fortunately, advocates in the United States did succeed in removing some of the barriers. Immediately after Lithuania fell to the USSR and France fell to Germany, groups such as the American Federation of Labor, the Vaad ha-Hatzala, and Agudath Israel of America (an international organization of Orthodox Jews) petitioned the State Department in Washington that special allowances be made for refugees believed to be in particular danger in Soviet- or Nazi-occupied territory. As a result, a limited number of nonquota visas were issued under the emergency visa program, as it became known. In the program's first six months, the State Department authorized 2,583 visas outside the quotas to applicants throughout occupied Europe. More than 700 were allotted to Jewish rabbis and Torah scholars. After that, few additional candidates were considered.[6]

In Lithuania, there was simply too little time between the enactment of the emergency visa program and the closure of the consulate to help the mass of applicants. During those few weeks, the American consul, Bernard Gufler, was able to complete

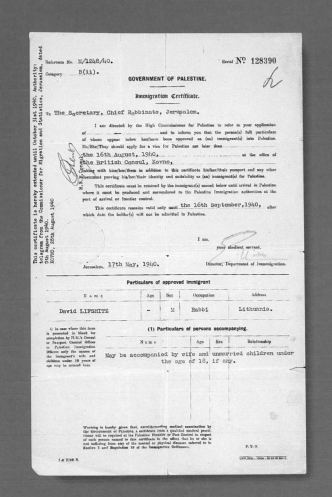

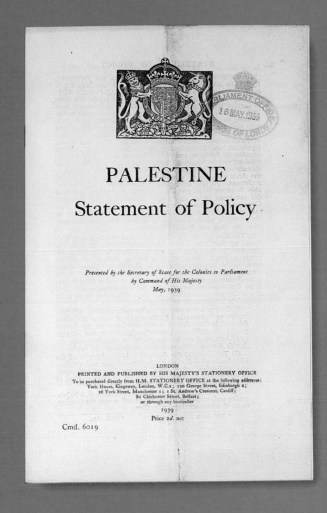

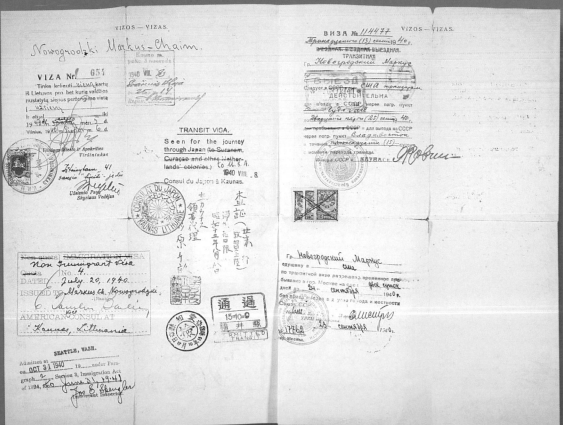

ABOVE LEFT: Palestine immigration certificate issued to Rabbi and Mrs. David Lifszyc in Kaunas, May 17, 1940. *Family of Rabbi David and Zipporah Lifshitz, New York*

ABOVE RIGHT: A British white paper issued May 17, 1939, restricted Jewish immigration to Palestine. *House of Lords Record Office, London*

LEFT: Non-immigration visa for the United States (bottom, far left) obtained by Markus Nowogrodzki in Kaunas in July 1940. Only a few dozen such visas were issued before the consulate closed in mid-August 1940. *Markus Nowogrodzki, New York*

When Dutch Ambassador L. P. J. de Decker authorized Jan Zwartendijk, the Dutch acting consul in Kaunas, to issue deceptive "Curaçao visas" in 1940, he was nearing the end of a diplomatic career that began in 1913. Born in Belgium, de Decker served in posts in Düsseldorf, Bucharest, Copenhagen, Hamburg, Yokohama, Hong Kong, and Bangkok. Sent to Riga, Latvia, in 1939, he was given the title "Extraordinary Representative and Minister." His wife died in Riga the same year. The de Deckers had no children.

After closing his Riga consulate in August 1940, de Decker left for Stockholm. He was subsequently posted in Yugoslavia, London, and Athens. De Decker died in 1948, leaving behind no comment on his decisive role in providing the "Curaçao visas."

only 55 such visas that covered 83 people.[7] Markus Nowogrodzki was one refugee who received an emergency visa. His father, Emanuel Nowogrodzki, a Bundist leader, was in New York on business when war broke out. He enlisted the help of the Jewish Labor Committee to secure emergency visas for both his son and his Bundist colleagues. Hundreds of others, even those with sponsorship, still had no destination visas.

Against this backdrop of blocked escape routes and rapid political change in Lithuania, the actions of three consular representatives stand out. The Dutch acting consul in Kaunas, Jan Zwartendijk, his superior in Riga, Ambassador L. P. J. de Decker, and the Japanese acting consul in Kaunas, Chiune Sugihara, responded compassionately to the refugee crisis created by the German war and Soviet occupation. These men supplied the necessary destination and transit visas that enabled the refugees to leave Lithuania on a journey none could have anticipated.

THE DECEPTION: HELP FROM THE DUTCH

In the summer of 1940, Pessla and Isaac Lewin were living in Vilna. Like many refugees, they were desperate to flee. Raised in the Netherlands, Pessla had given up her Dutch citizenship in 1935 when she married Isaac, a Polish Jew. Nevertheless, she wrote a letter to Ambassador de Decker petitioning to enter the Dutch West Indies. With de Decker's consent, she mailed him her passport, in which he noted on July 11 that "for the admission of aliens to Surinam, Curaçao, and other Dutch possessions in the Americas, an entry visa is not required."[8]

De Decker's notation was a conscious deceit. He intentionally omitted the clause stipulating that entry to the Dutch West Indies required the permission of local colonial governors. De Decker also knew that this permission was granted only on rare occasions. But the diplomatic notation in Pessla Lewin's passport gave the appearance of an authoritative directive and a final destination. The Dutch ambassador's

written "permission" to enter Curaçao was no more than a bluff—but it offered a means of escape.

Eleven days later in Kaunas, Isaac Lewin showed his wife's passport with de Decker's notation to Acting Consul Zwartendijk. Zwartendijk copied the notation into Lewin's safe-conduct document.[9] Soon afterward, three Dutch students from the Telz Yeshiva in Lithuania—Nathan Gutwirth, Chaim Nussbaum, and Levi Sternheim, Pessla Lewin's brother—asked Zwartendijk for the same notation, that a visa was not required for entering the Dutch possessions in the Caribbean. Zwartendijk, the director of the Dutch radio manufacturer Philips in Lithuania who had assumed the duties of acting consul only a few weeks earlier, was not sure how to respond.[10] "Since the [consular] manual did not provide a clear answer," he recalled, "I asked de Decker by mail what the possibilities were. In his answer I received the instructions what I could enter in the passport of the applicant"—the same incomplete

OPPOSITE: Dutch Ambassador L. P. J. de Decker issued this "Curaçao visa" in Riga on July 11, 1940, to Pessla Lewin, a former Dutch citizen married to a Polish Jewish refugee. *Isaac Lewin, Remember the Days of Old (New York: Research Institute of Religious Jewry, 1994)*

OPPOSITE, RIGHT: Jan Zwartendijk with his daughter, Edith, and son, Jan Jr., Kaunas, Lithuania, 1940. *The Zwartendijk Family*

OPPOSITE, BOTTOM: Radio manufactured in Lithuania in 1937 by the Dutch company Philips, whose director in that country was Jan Zwartendijk. *USHMM*

BELOW: Handbook for the Dutch consular service, similar to the one used by Acting Consul Jan Zwartendijk to learn about visa procedures. *Netherlands Ministry of Foreign Affairs, The Hague*

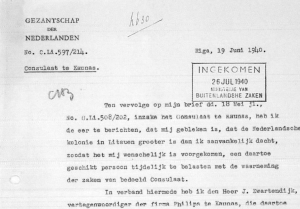

ABOVE: On June 19, 1940, Ambassador L. P. J. de Decker informed the Netherlands Foreign Ministry in exile in London that he was appointing Dutch businessman Jan Zwartendijk acting consul in Kaunas, Lithuania. *Netherlands Ministry of Foreign Affairs, The Hague*

In December 1938, Jan Zwartendijk arrived in Kaunas, where he became the director of the Lithuanian branch of Philips, a large Dutch manufacturer of light bulbs and radios. The company's operations, including a busy workshop of 20 employees, were disrupted in the spring of 1940 after Germany's invasion of the Netherlands prevented the export of radio components to Lithuania.

In June 1940, Ambassador L. P. J. de Decker asked Zwartendijk to serve as acting consul in Lithuania, replacing the ethnic German who resigned following the German occupation of the Netherlands. With characteristic modesty, Zwartendijk initially demurred, but he accepted the post after de Decker reassured him that his duties would be limited. Soon afterward, Zwartendijk unwittingly found himself with the authority to play a pivotal role in the lives of refugees desperate to leave Lithuania.

Only decades after the war did Zwartendijk learn that the "visas" he had issued in Kaunas had enabled hundreds of refugees to flee Soviet territory. Many of the recipients of these "visas" forgot his name or never learned it. To them, he became the "Angel of Curaçao" or "Mr. Philips Radio." He probably would have been uncomfortable with the former title. To the end of his life, he maintained that if anyone deserved credit for initiating the

(continued on p. 63)

PHOTO: *USHMM, courtesy of the Zwartendijk Family*

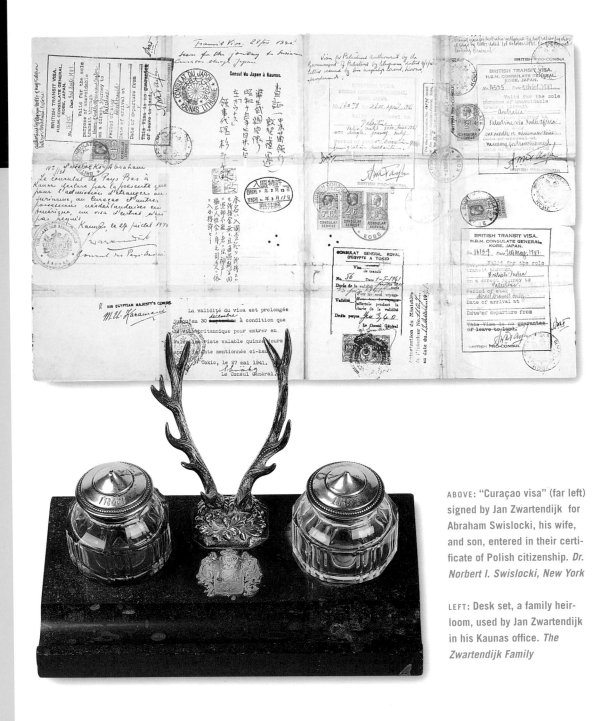

ABOVE: "Curaçao visa" (far left) signed by Jan Zwartendijk for Abraham Swislocki, his wife, and son, entered in their certificate of Polish citizenship. *Dr. Norbert I. Swislocki, New York*

LEFT: Desk set, a family heirloom, used by Jan Zwartendijk in his Kaunas office. *The Zwartendijk Family*

language used in Pessla Lewin's passport. "For sure," Zwartendijk continued, "it was not an up to par entrance *visum*."[11]

News of the so-called Curaçao visas circulated quickly in the tight-knit world of refugees. Some of them dismissed as a joke the scheme to seek destination visas to this unknown Caribbean island. Others, although skeptical about the likelihood of success, grasped at any opportunity to get away. By the hundreds, they made the short

train trip from Vilna to Zwartendijk's office in Kaunas.[12] Maks and Zofia Sztejn and their two children heard about these "visas" from other refugees they met on the street. Although they had no idea where they would end up, they secured the sought-after documents anyway in the hope they would provide a way out.[13]

Zwartendijk's postwar recollections suggest he had little faith that the Curaçao notations would secure the refugees' freedom.

He nonetheless worked feverishly to fulfill all requests. At first he wrote and signed each visa by hand; he soon had a rubber stamp made that replaced his handwritten notations, making them look more official. The charge for each was 11 litas (about two dollars).[14] An exact list of "visa" recipients does not exist, because de Decker ordered Zwartendijk to burn his consular records to prevent their falling into Soviet hands. But travel documents with stamps dated July 22 to August 2, 1940, and numbered as high as 2,400 have been identified.[15]

Zwartendijk was not the only Dutch consul to use de Decker's abbreviated "Curaçao visas" (the "visa" de Decker issued to Pessla Lewin is the only known notation he personally signed). After closing the Riga embassy, de Decker went to Sweden, where he described the Curaçao scheme to A. M. de Jong, the Dutch consul in Stockholm. Telegrams, letters, and photographs soon began to arrive in Sweden from Lithuania and the other Baltic countries. Like Zwartendijk, de Jong was well aware that the declaration would not provide entry to Curaçao, but he nonetheless mailed some 400 "visas" in early 1941.[16] Unfortunately, for various reasons including the late date of issuance, most of his notations were never used.

The Dutch diplomats' motivation to issue "Curaçao visas" is difficult to ascertain since de Decker said nothing about the episode after the war, and Zwartendijk spoke little of the matter. De Jong's postwar testimony, however, provides a clue. The idea for the "visas," he stated, originally was based on the experience of Dutch refugees in Scan-

(continued from p. 62)

unexpected chain of events, it was de Decker, "who delivered . . . the successful text for the *pseudovisum*."

For his efforts on behalf of the refugees in Kaunas, Zwartendijk was posthumously honored, in 1997, as "Righteous Among the Nations" by Yad Vashem, the Israeli Holocaust Remembrance Authority.

ABOVE: **A. M. de Jong, Dutch consul-general, Stockholm, 1941.** *Netherlands Institute for War Documentation (NIOD), Amsterdam*

RIGHT: **"Curaçao visa" signed by A. M. de Jong, January 25, 1941, and mailed to Leiba Pruski in Lithuania.** *Netherlands Ministry of Foreign Affairs, The Hague*

Chiune Sugihara
(1900–1986)

Chiune Sugihara, raised in a middle-class family, graduated from the exclusive Harbin Gakuin, Japan's training center for Russia experts. He resided in Harbin, Manchuria, for 16 years, where he learned fluent Russian from émigrés, including his first wife during their six-year marriage. As the director of the Foreign Ministry in Manchukuo (where Japan set up a puppet government after it occupied Manchuria), Sugihara helped negotiate the purchase of the North Manchurian Railroad from the Soviet Union in 1932. Three years later he returned to Tokyo, where he wed Yukiko Kikuchi, and they started a family.

Sugihara spent a little less than a year in Kaunas. After the Soviets forced him to close the consulate in 1940, he went briefly to Berlin and then to Prague and Königsberg. He slowly worked his way up the ranks of second-tier diplomats, advancing from being the only Japanese diplomat in Kaunas to having two Japanese subordinates at the legation in Bucharest, Romania, where he served from 1942 until 1944. At the end of the war, the Red Army arrested Sugihara with other enemy diplomats in their zone of occupation. He and his family were held under relatively benign conditions until they were repatriated in 1947.

When Sugihara returned to Japan, he was retired with a small pension

(continued on p. 65)

PHOTO: *USHMM, courtesy of Hiroki Sugihara*

dinavia who wished to join their national military under the command of the Dutch government-in-exile in London. The USSR prohibited these Dutch nationals from transiting Soviet territory to reach any British destination because permission to do so would violate the Soviets' non-aggression pact with Germany. The USSR could, however, allow transit to reach Dutch possessions in the East or West Indies. De Jong also testified: "We in Sweden, who enjoyed the privilege of living in freedom, felt obliged to find possibilities to help everyone who was trying to escape from the area of the tyrants."[17]

THE CHAIN REACTION: SUGIHARA VISAS

In issuing the "Curaçao visas," de Decker and Zwartendijk set off an "unexpected chain reaction."[18] Warhaftig recalled that when he learned about the notations, he "looked at the map and saw that the way to Curaçao was through the USSR to Vladivostok, from there to Japan. From Japan by boat to Curaçao, through the Panama

Canal."[19] Although the plan seemed far-fetched, many refugees were undeterred. Hoping to acquire Japanese transit visas and then approach the Soviets for exit visas, they took their Curaçao notations to Japan's acting consul, Chiune Sugihara.

Sugihara was dispatched to Kaunas in November 1939 to set up his nation's first consulate in Lithuania. He arrived with his wife, Yukiko, her sister, and his two young sons, and he rented a white stucco house on a hilly street that provided a view of downtown Kaunas. The consular offices were on the ground floor, his family's apartment above. From there, Acting Consul Sugihara began his service as Japan's "eyes" in the region, reporting on German and Soviet troop movements along the border.[20] Even though a signatory of the Anti-Comintern Pact with Germany in 1936, Japan pursued an independent foreign policy, including recognizing the Polish government-in-exile in London, members of whose underground regularly offered intelligence to Sugihara. One recalled providing him with "information about Soviet preparations on the

(continued from p. 64)

as part of the Foreign Ministry's general reduction in force during the American occupation. He then held a variety of jobs, including representing a Japanese trading company in Moscow from 1960 to 1975. A year before his death in 1986, Yad Vashem honored Sugihara as "Righteous Among the Nations" for his aid to Jewish refugees in Lithuania during World War II.

OPPOSITE: Chiune Sugihara at home in Kaunas with his family, c. 1940. From left to right: his wife's sister Setsuko, his sons Chiaki and Hiroki, and his wife, Yukiko. *USHMM, courtesy of Hiroki Sugihara*

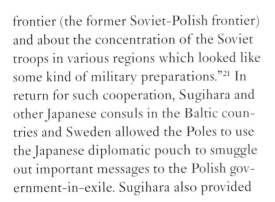

ABOVE: Chiune Sugihara (second from left), with some of his Polish underground contacts and their families at the Kaunas train station, c. 1940. *USHMM, courtesy of Hiroki Sugihara*

RIGHT: Refugees seeking transit visas wait outside the Japanese consulate, Kaunas, July 27, 1940. *USHMM, courtesy of Hiroki Sugihara*

frontier (the former Soviet-Polish frontier) and about the concentration of the Soviet troops in various regions which looked like some kind of military preparations."[21] In return for such cooperation, Sugihara and other Japanese consuls in the Baltic countries and Sweden allowed the Poles to use the Japanese diplomatic pouch to smuggle out important messages to the Polish government-in-exile. Sugihara also provided his Polish underground contacts with transit visas through Japan.

One morning in late July 1940, Sugihara awoke to an unusual noise outside the consulate. "There were people outside and they were talking very loudly. I went to the window of my apartment and looked out to find what was going on. I saw a crowd of Polish refugees behind the fences. . . .

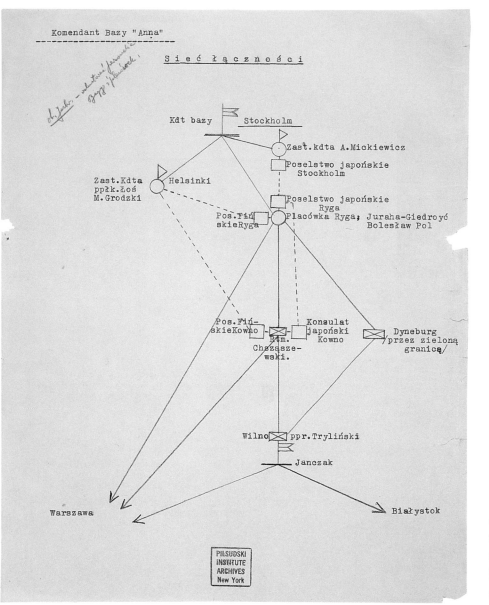

Komendant Bazy "Anna"

S i e ć   ł ą c z n o ś c i

Kdt bazy   Stockholm

                    Zast.kdta A.Mickiewicz

                    Poselstwo japońskie
                         Stockholm

Zast.Kdta   Helsinki
ppłk.Łoś
M.Grodzki   Poselstwo japońskie
                         Ryga
        Pos.Fiń-   Placówka Ryga; Juraha-Giedroyć
        skieRyga   Bolesław Pol

        Pos.Fiń-   Konsulat   Dyneburg
        skieKowno   japoński   /przez zieloną
                Rtm.   Kowno   granicę/
                Chszasze-
                wski.

                Wilno   ppr.Tryliński

                    Janczak

Warszawa   Białystok

PILSUDSKI
INSTITUTE
ARCHIVES
New York

Diagram showing "the web of communications" between Japanese diplomats and members of the Polish Resistance in the Baltic States and Scandinavia. The "Konsulat japonski Kowno" (center) refers to Chiune Sugihara. *Pilsudski Institute Archives, New York*

Each day the crowd grew bigger."[22] The refugees pleaded for Japanese transit visas to open the way for them to leave Lithuania eastward across the Soviet Union to Japan.

On July 28, Sugihara cabled a dramatic description of the urgent situation in occupied Lithuania to the Japanese foreign minister, Yosuke Matsuoka:

> The Communists' power in this country is rapidly expanding. Under the influence of the GPU [a branch of the Soviet NKVD], many acts of terrorism are occurring. At first, the GPU arriving with the Red

Army attacked the headquarters of political parties of the Poles, White Russians, people of this country, and Jews.... In Vilna they have imprisoned 1,500 ... and 2,000 from other areas.... Most of them are members of the Polish military government, White Russian military officers, and members of the ruling party of the old administrative power of this country. Socialists, Bundists, Zionists, and other Jews, and the former prime minister, Merukus, and Foreign Minister Rupischitz with their families were all sent to Moscow. And in the past week, 1,600 Poles have been sent to Samara. Because of this the British government here has been protesting to the Russians. As this has been happening, many have felt the danger and have escaped to the outskirts but only a few have been successful in getting back to the German territory. The number of runaways to Germany is said to be several hundred. Every day nearly 100 people are coming and Jews throng to our building asking for visas to go to the U.S. via Japan.[23]

Sugihara's superiors in Tokyo were slow to answer his cable. While waiting for their response, Sugihara took it upon himself to begin issuing hundreds of visas. In English and Japanese, they read: "TRANSIT-VISA. Seen for the journey *through Japan* (to Suranam [*sic*], Curaçao and other Netherlands colonies)." For each, Sugihara charged a standard fee of two litas (about 35 cents).[24] He later wrote: "I finally decided that it was completely useless to continue the discussions with Tokyo, I was merely losing time.... I gave visas to all who came to me, regardless of the fact whether or not they could produce some kind of document proving they were going to another country."[25]

Most of the refugees who approached Sugihara did have a sort of destination visa—the Curaçao notation from Zwartendijk. Although the two men never met, for a brief

ABOVE: Leon Ilutovich's "Curaçao visa" (bottom, far left), issued on July 31, 1940, and Japanese transit visa (top, left center) added two days later. Both were entered on his certificate of Polish citizenship. *USHMM, Gift of Rebeka Ilutovich*

LEFT: Cable from Foreign Minister Yosuke Matsuoka, Tokyo, to Acting Consul Chiune Sugihara, Kaunas, August 16, 1940, instructing him to issue visas only to refugees who had fulfilled the entry requirements. *Japanese Foreign Ministry Diplomatic Record Office, Tokyo*

period in the summer of 1940 they became an unofficial team. Years later, Zwartendijk recalled with wry amusement that during the eight-day period when they were both issuing visas, he received telephone calls from Sugihara imploring him to slow down: "He could not keep up, the street was full of waiting people."[26] Sugihara issued visas at a furious pace, stamping as many as 260 in a single day, the bulk while Zwartendijk was still issuing Curaçao notations.[27] He continued to approve visas for more than three weeks after Zwartendijk closed his office on August 2, though the number of visas issued gradually decreased. The dates on most refugees' papers indicate a lag between Zwartendijk's Curaçao notations and Sugihara's transit visas, but some refugees managed to obtain both in short order.

To keep up with demand, Sugihara departed from diplomatic protocol and accepted help from an outsider. Moshe Zupnik and four other Mir Yeshiva students had trekked to Kaunas to get visas for the entire yeshiva once its spiritual leader, Rabbi Eliezer Finkel, agreed to a mass emigration. After obtaining 300 "Curaçao visas" from Zwartendijk, the five yeshiva students headed for the Japanese consulate. There Zupnik met with Wolfgang Gudze, the consulate's ethnic German secretary, who introduced him to Sugihara. Communicating in broken English, Sugihara asked how the students planned to fund their trip through Japan. Zupnik assured him that Rabbi Abraham Kalmanowitz, Mir Yeshiva's representative in New York, would guarantee their passage. When the skeptical Sugihara asked for proof, Zupnik bluffed: "We are against communism and are considered enemies of the state, and we must leave in secret; we have a code, and cannot write officially." The answer satisfied Sugihara, who agreed not only to issue visas to the entire group but also to let Zupnik help process them.[28] For two weeks, Zupnik (who spoke German) worked side by side with Gudze. At times their cooperation was so efficient that it took on the character of an assembly line. Visa applicants did not even have to enter the house; they could stand on the porch and receive visas through a window.

Sugihara's initiative to issue the transit visas was lauded by the Polish ambassador to Tokyo, Tadeusz Romer. Reporting to his government-in-exile in London, Romer wrote:

> Polish citizens, both Poles and Jews, who are here highly praise the Japanese consular offices in Kaunas and the help they received from this office.... Many of our compatriots owe their survival to the personal sacrifice of Japanese personnel who went above and beyond the customary, rigid, and bureaucratic regulations.

LEFT: Mir Yeshiva student Moshe Zupnik, who helped process visas at the Japanese consulate in Kaunas. *Rabbi Moshe Zupnik, New York*

BELOW: List of transit visas issued in Lithuania by Sugihara from July 11 to August 31, 1940. The list he sent from Prague in 1941 to the Japanese Foreign Ministry contained 2,140 names. *Japanese Foreign Ministry Diplomatic Record Office, Tokyo*

Behavior of other foreign legations in Kaunas stood in sharp contrast to that, according to what I heard.[29]

When Sugihara decided to issue the transit visas on the strength of the Curaçao notations, he loosely interpreted Foreign Ministry protocols, but he did not defy them outright. There was no reason for him to believe he should not honor the Dutch documents since Japan recognized the Dutch government-in-exile after the Netherlands had fallen to Germany. He might or might not have known that the "Curaçao visas" were a ruse, though he certainly was aware that most refugees were not interested in going to Curaçao. In his July 28 cable to the Foreign Ministry, he remarked that the refugees were approaching him for permission to go to the United States by way of Japan.[30] In any case, the "Curaçao visas" served their purpose: they provided what his government required before issuing anyone permission to travel through Japan.

In mid-August 1940, the first refugees carrying Sugihara visas began to reach Japan. Their arrival, often without money or final-destination visas, prompted the Foreign Ministry in Tokyo to cable Sugihara at least four times reiterating standard procedures. In the third and most strongly worded cable, dated August 16, the ministry instructed Sugihara: "You must make sure that they have finished their procedure for their entry visas and also they must possess the travel money that they need during their stay in Japan. Otherwise, you should not give them the transit visa."[31] By the time Sugihara received this cable, however, he had already issued some 1,800 visas. After receiving the August 16 cable from Tokyo, Sugihara qualified his transit visas by noting in each refugee's identity papers: "The applicant stated that (s)he knew that (s)he should obtain permission to enter the destination countries beyond Japan and complete reservations for a boarding pass before boarding at Vladivostok, and this visa was issued."[32]

On about September 1, Sugihara further explained to Tokyo the extenuating circumstances under which he was issuing visas: Japan was the only transit country available for going "in the direction of the United States" (he did not mention Curaçao), and his visas were needed in order to leave the Soviet Union. As justification for his actions, Sugihara argued that the refugees could presumably finalize their destination plans at the foreign embassies in Moscow or the consulates in Vladivostok. Should they arrive at the Soviet port of Vladivostok with incomplete paperwork, he suggested, they simply should not be allowed to board a ship for Japan.[33] Tokyo, concerned that turning away the refugees would damage faith in Japanese visas, cabled back immediately: "The shipping company cannot deny the person who holds our transit visa [permission to board] at Vladivostok." Moreover, the Soviets insisted that holders of Japanese transit visas move on to Japan, and the Japanese had little choice but to comply. (It is unlikely that Sugihara even saw this reply from the Foreign Ministry because the cable arrived in Kaunas on September 4, the day the acting consul left Lithuania for Berlin.)[34]

Sugihara issued visas as late as August 31, 1940—the day he closed the consulate. Among the last to get the coveted transit visas were members of the Sztejn family. Bianca Sztejn Lloyd recalled that Sugihara continued to issue visas even while workers were removing furniture and boxes from the consulate.[35]

Sugihara stands out among Japanese diplomats stationed in Europe at the time, not because he issued transit visas to the refugees—his colleagues also did that—but because he issued so many, so quickly, even to people technically not qualified to obtain them. In February 1941, by which time hundreds of the refugees had arrived in Japan, the Foreign Ministry cabled Sugihara—then posted as acting consul general in

Prague and continuing to issue transit visas to Jews—asking him to document the number of visas he had issued in Kaunas and how many of the recipients were Jews. Sugihara promptly cabled back that he had issued 2,132 visas, of which an estimated 1,500 went to Jews.[36]

A comparison of Sugihara's own list with the recorded names of refugees who arrived in Japan shows that he did not significantly underreport the number of visas he issued. More than 2,000 Polish Jews and a small number of refugees of other nationalities are documented as having reached Japan. The names of several hundred of those who arrived in Japan do not appear on the list Sugihara sent to the Foreign Ministry, because some had arrived with forged documents and others had visas issued by other Japanese consuls in Europe. Sugihara did overestimate the number of non-Jews who

received visas from him. Few non-Jewish Polish citizens ever reached Japan, and at most several dozen, rather than the hundreds Sugihara mentioned, actually received his visas.

Lists of people who arrived in Japan with Sugihara visas bring to light some other facts hidden behind the numbers. First, as many as 30 refugees, including Zorach Warhaftig, received more than one visa, either in order to stamp different identity documents or to coordinate with different destination visas on a single document. Second, several hundred people received visas who, for various reasons, were unable to leave Lithuania. For example, Oskar Schenker and his brother Alfred reached Japan, but their mother, wives, and their children were never able to take advantage of the visas secured for them; before they could even reach Vilna, they were deported

Port of Vladivostok, where Soviet authorities insisted that refugees holding Japanese transit visas board ships for Japan—even if they had not completed all the necessary arrangements for proceeding to destinations beyond. *National Archives and Records Administration, Washington, D.C.*

from Soviet-occupied Poland to the Soviet interior.[37] And third, a single document could save several people. Some 300 people, mostly children, reached Japan on visas issued to other family members.

In March 1941, Tokyo cabled the other Japanese diplomats stationed in Europe, requesting the total number of transit visas each had issued. They responded with much more modest numbers than Sugihara had. Over the course of the preceding 13 months, Japanese diplomats in Hamburg issued 1,414 visas; in Vienna, 786; in Berlin, 691; in Stockholm, 338; and in Moscow, 152.[38] Like Sugihara, they had been advised to ensure that anyone seeking to transit Japan had destination visas and adequate funds for the journey. Reports on the arrival of Austrian and German Jews in Japan indicate that most of them, unlike those from Lithuania, arrived with their paperwork complete, transited briefly, and then continued on to their final destinations.[39]

JAPANESE POLICY TOWARD THE JEWS

Japan drifted toward the German camp politically during the 1930s, but for both powers, an alliance was more the result of global geopolitical considerations than of shared ideology. Although Japanese leaders had signed the Anti-Comintern Pact with Germany, they did not believe it should influence treatment of their tiny Jewish population or of the Jewish refugees who intended to pass through Japan.[40] Even after September 1940, when Japan signed the Tripartite Pact that formalized its alliance with Germany and Italy, the Japanese government continued to pursue its own policy toward Jews.

Historically, antisemitism barely figured in the Japanese consciousness, as most Japanese had no daily contact with Jews. Anti-Jewish ideas had reached Japan after the Siberian campaigns of the Russian Revolution. Japanese officers, having adopted a crude form of antisemitism from their White Russian counterparts, promoted themselves as Jewish "experts" and translated into Japanese "The Protocols of the Elders of Zion," an antisemitic forgery that depicts an imaginary worldwide Jewish conspiracy. However, these translations were never widely circulated, and the tract's underlying antisemitism did not spread.

Japan's first encounter with large numbers of Jews came in the 1930s, when refugees from Nazism began to arrive in Japan en route to final destinations. Between 1933 and 1941, German policy encouraged Jewish emigration from the Reich, but until 1938, few wanted to go to the Far East if other destinations were available. All that changed after the *Anschluss,* Germany's annexation of Austria in March 1938, and *Kristallnacht,* the organized, nationwide violence against the German Jews and their property in November 1938. Jews, now desperate to leave the Reich, were willing to consider destinations as unlikely as the Japanese-controlled port of Shanghai, China.

Under pressure to establish a coherent Jewish policy because of increasing Jewish

Foreign Minister Yosuke Matsuoka meeting with Hitler six months after Japan, Germany, and Italy were aligned in the Tripartite Pact, March 27, 1941. *Imperial War Museum, London*

demands to enter Japan and its empire, the nation's top five governmental ministers (the prime minister, foreign minister, finance minister, and ministers of the army and navy) convened in December 1938. The Five Ministers Conference declared: "As a rule," Japan should "avoid actively embracing Jews who are expelled by its allies." To do so would not be "in the spirit of the empire's long-standing advocacy of racial equality."[41] While Japanese policy generally opposed the entry of any foreigner, the ministers also stated that Jews seeking to enter Japan in the future would be allowed the same rights of brief transit granted to others. Soon after the Five Ministers Conference, the Foreign Ministry sent its overseas embassies a statement that echoed the conclusion reached at the meeting: adopting an anti-Jewish stance was not in Japan's best interest.[42]

A crucial provision of the Five Ministers document stipulated the particular importance of not estranging Jews because of Japan's "need to invite foreign capital, particularly for economic development," and its desire "to avoid worsening relations with the United States."[43] In the late 1930s, an influential faction in Japan's government, overestimating the political and financial power of American Jews, calculated that the country's benevolent treatment of Jews would counteract anti-Japanese opinion in the United States. They also hoped that politically well-placed Jews would intervene on Japan's behalf with leaders in Washington who, in 1938, had placed an embargo on exports of aviation fuel to Japan.

Japan also sought to lure Jews—notably wealthy capitalists and industrialists—to the territories it occupied in sparsely settled Manchuria. Japanese policymakers estimated that an infusion of money and technical know-how would give the region's economy a much-needed boost. Although plans to settle Jews in Manchuria never took

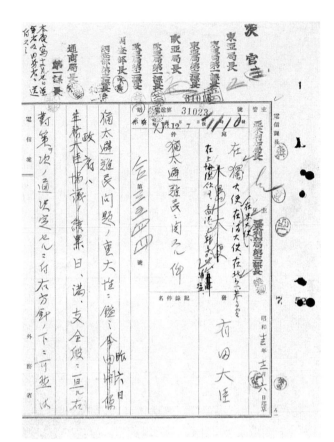

on the status of official policy, Japanese emissaries encouraged Jews to invest there. In November 1940, for example, Bernhard Kahn of the Joint's New York office reported on a visit from Kozo Tamura, a wealthy Japanese industrialist, who sought "to persuade Jewish organizations here to present some scheme for helping Jews to settle in Japan or Japanese controlled Manchuria."[44]

Japan's pragmatic approach to the Jews as potential peace-brokers, financiers, and settlers helps explain the country's tolerance of the refugees who arrived on its shores in 1940 and 1941. Most of the Jewish refugees who made their way to Japan in late 1940 and early 1941 had transit visas, issued by Sugihara in Kaunas, that permitted them to stay for only about ten days. Nonetheless, the majority remained in Japan much longer, some departing just weeks before the Japanese attack on Pearl Harbor and the outbreak of the Pacific war.

Cable from Japanese Foreign Minister Hachiro Arita to all Japanese embassies, December 7, 1938, informing them of the policy toward Jews formulated by the Five Ministers Conference. *Japanese Foreign Ministry Diplomatic Record Office, Tokyo*

THE TRANS-SIBERIAN EXPRESS

INTOURIST MOSCOW USSR

5 JOURNEY

THE DOOR OPENS

The refugees who held Sugihara visas and the Dutch "Curaçao visas" knew the documents were worthless scraps of paper if they could not first leave Soviet Lithuania. The question of emigrating from Soviet territory, previously "unheard of," troubled even Sugihara.[1] When the hopeful émigrés began requesting transit visas, he made inquiries to see if the Soviets would approve transit visas for the journey across the USSR. "The Soviet consulate," he later reported, "made it clear that they were prepared to issue transit visas provided they had the correct Japanese visas."[2] Sometime in August 1940, the Soviets unexpectedly consented and began to process refugee exit applications.

Soviet motivations for issuing exit visas to the refugees remain unknown. Did the appeals by advocates of the Jewish refugees during the summer of 1940 convince Soviet authorities that foreigners could not be assimilated into the Soviet economy and therefore should be allowed to leave? Did the requirement that transportation out of the country be purchased with dollars offer a sufficiently valuable supply of much-needed hard currency? Did the Soviets intend to plant NKVD agents among the refugees? More than one émigré later recounted Soviet interrogators' attempts to induce them to spy, but none who refused were prevented from leaving. Whatever

the truth, departure from Soviet Lithuania was now possible.

The procedure for securing an exit permit involved an interview with the NKVD. Soviet interrogators could be demanding one moment, or brief and dismissive the next. A meeting might last only a few minutes, or a refugee might be summoned back repeatedly over the course of several weeks. The inconsistencies could be terrifying, but in some ways worked to the refugees' advantage. Tadeusz Romer, the Polish ambassador to Japan, learned about the tortuous application process from refugees who finally reached the Far East: "The inquisitorial investigation of the police prevailed together with an indescribable chaos."

Menorah smuggled out of Suwalki, Poland, by Rabbi David Lifszyc, who carried it with him on the Trans-Siberian Railroad journey to Japan in 1941. *Family of Rabbi David and Zipporah Lifshitz, New York*

The last peculiarity however afforded to more than one his chance of success, who under other circumstances would certainly not have been authorized to leave."[3]

Applying to the NKVD for exit permits was known to be a gamble. A trip to see Zwartendijk or Sugihara might, at worst, result in some wasted time, but an appeal to the Soviets could mean arrest and deportation. The refugees simply could not believe that the Soviets, with no history of leniency, would freely issue so many exit permits without having a "devilish plan."[4] Leaders of yeshivas that had fled to Lithuania were especially fearful of exposing

their students to Soviet scrutiny. Many discouraged large-scale attempts to flee, and the students generally followed their lead. On the other hand, refugees were encouraged when reports from Vladivostok indicated that the first groups of travelers had arrived there safely.[5]

At all hours of the day and night, refugees waiting for interviews clogged the corridors of the NKVD headquarters. The interviewers made no effort to keep normal office hours, often summoning an exhausted applicant in the middle of the night. The hopeful émigrés took calculated risks to go home to steal some much-needed sleep; if their names came up while they were gone, they forfeited their place in line and were forced to begin anew.[6]

The NKVD interview was incomplete without a detailed questionnaire and an "autobiography" to explain why the refugee wanted to leave the Soviet Union. Like all other dealings with the Soviets, submitting the autobiography could be hazardous. It was necessary to strike a careful balance between presenting truthful information that could disqualify them and fabricating bold lies that might be exposed. Some refugees chose to prevaricate. Josef Mlotek, the son of a rabbi and a member of the Bund who worked for the Bundist newspaper *Folkstsaytung,* identified himself as a textile manufacturer in his autobiographical statement. Fearing persecution because of his Bundist past, he mentioned nothing of this in his statement.[7] Whether his past was known or not, his bluff worked, and he received an exit permit and made his way across the Soviet Union safely. In other cases, the simple truth seemed to work. Rabbi David Lifszyc wrote in his statement: "I am not suited to any other work since my whole life has been devoted to rabbinical

training and to carrying out rabbinical duties. For that reason, I am unable to settle here."[8] Allowed to depart, he, his wife, and five-year-old daughter escaped to San Francisco, arriving in May 1941.

After the often terrifying interview and the lengthy application procedure, in which each word had to be measured and each statement carefully considered, the refugees waited to see if permission had been granted. The wait could be just as dreadful as the application procedure itself. Benjamin Fishoff later remembered

those cold winter nights when hundreds of people stood in the corridors of the Russian emigration office, waiting for the posting of the list containing the names of those who had received exit permits. We were full of mixed feelings of happiness and deep worry. Would we arrive in peace or was this not just another Soviet trick to discover who wanted to escape their "Garden of Eden"? More than a few of us worried about the possibility that during our trip the train would stop in Siberia, for several years.[9]

Reserved railroad pass for travel from Moscow to Vladivostok. It was used by one of the few refugees who paid for the trans-Siberian passage with rubles and without going through the Soviet Intourist agency.
Stefan Golston, Washington

JOURNEY

$1,000,000

CASH RECEIPT No. 2233

HIAS
RESCUE THRU EMIGRATION
Campaign

HEBREW SHELTERING AND IMMIGRANT AID SOCIETY
425 LAFAYETTE STREET — ALgonquin 4-2900 — NEW YORK

RECEIVED
NOTED BY   REFER TO
MAL
JAN 18 1941   HKB
ANSWERED

Jan. 17, 1941

Mr. Moses Leavitt, Secy.
Joint Distribution Committee
100 East 42nd Street
New York City

Dear Moe:

    Following the conversation you had
with me yesterday concerning the emigration of
a substantial number of our people from
Vilnius, we are pleased to send you herewith
our check No. 549 in the amount of $10,000
as the Hias contribution toward the transportation expenses.

Very sincerely yours

Isaac L. Asofsky
EXECUTIVE DIRECTOR

AG
Encl

30060

ACT NOW

CAMPAIGN OFFICERS
HON. MITCHELL MAY
  Chairman
MAURICE LEVIN
ALBERT ROSENBLATT
MAX J. SCHNEIDER
  Co-Chairmen
JOHN L. BERNSTEIN
MORRIS FEINSTONE
ABRAHAM HERMAN
  Vice-Chairmen
H. FISCHEL
  Treasurer
NATHAN SCHOENFELD
  Associate Treasurer
ISAAC L. ASOFSKY
  Secretary

PLAN and SCOPE COMMITTEE
SAMUEL A. TELSEY
  Chairman
EDWARD M. BENTON
S. DINGOL
HON. JONAH J. GOLDSTEIN
SAMUEL GOLDSTEIN
MURRAY I. GURFEIN
REUBEN GUSKIN
JACOB MASSEL
JOSEPH SCHLOSSBERG
BENJAMIN J. WEINBERG
  and Campaign Officers
ALBERT A. PETERS
  Campaign Director

BUSINESS MEN'S COUNCIL
JOSEPH PULVERMACHER
  Chairman

TRADE UNION COMMITTEE
JOSEPH SCHLOSSBERG
  Chairman

WOMEN'S DIVISION
MRS. LEON KAMAIKY
MRS. ABRAHAM HERMAN

FAR-EAST-EUROPE 12 DAYS.

The Trans-SIBERIAN Express

USSR State Tourist Company
"INTOURIST"
№ 10 Sanchome, Marunouchi,
Kojimachi-ky, Tokyo
Tel. Marunouchi 2307-09
Telegraph. Address
"Vneshtorg"

Head office Moskow,
Gorkii Street, 11.

Through Tickets
to
Europe via Siberia

Distributor

Tokyo, _____, 19____

№ _____

In her diary, Rose Shoshana Kahan also wrote about the anxieties of waiting:

> At the entrance of 12 Vilna Street are lined up several hundred refugees who wait for the lucky moment when they'll see their name among the lucky ones on the posted list giving the names of those who have received visas. This is how they spend entire days and part of the nights, waiting until the return home, disappointed, only to return there again the next morning. Perhaps their name will appear that day on the list.

If someone's name was spotted on the list and he or she was not there, "no attention is paid to the lateness of the hour at night, but haste is made to run and wake the person from sleep to tell them the good news." This is how Kahan and her husband, Lazar, learned that their names had been posted. She went to pick up their visas the next morning, while her husband went to Kaunas to buy train tickets.[10]

PAYING FOR PASSAGE

For many who had successfully run the gauntlet of Soviet requirements for exit visas, the next step seemed nearly impossible — meeting the Soviet requirement that the trans-Siberian trek be paid for with U.S. dollars. Tickets for the journey cost about $200 and had to be purchased from Intourist, the official Soviet government travel agency. The refugees faced a quandary. Since the incorporation of Lithuania into the USSR, it had been declared illegal for residents to possess foreign currency. Now, even if the refugees managed to come up with the staggering sum, possessing it was illegal. Ever resourceful, many took to carrying the money in envelopes marked "For the trip to Siberia," which they hoped would absolve them in the event they were caught and searched.[11]

Some refugees, like the Sondheimer family, managed to amass the necessary funds by appealing to sympathetic friends and relatives overseas.[12] Others traded money on the black market or dipped into emergency reserves. But the vast majority received at least part of the money from the Joint Distribution Committee.[13] In Vilna, the Joint's Moses Beckelman did everything in his power to help the refugees escape, even disregarding instructions from the Joint's home office. In November 1940, after scores of refugees with Sugihara transit visas had reached Japan, the Joint headquarters cabled its office in Lisbon:

> THESE PEOPLE HAVE CURACAO VISAS WHICH WE KNOW INVALID STOP PLEASE ADVISE BECKELMAN.[14]

Ten days later, Lisbon forwarded Beckelman's reply to New York:

> BECKELMAN AWARE UNVALIDITY CURACAO VISAS COMMENTS QUOTE NEVERTHELESS . . .

The names and addresses of Polish citizens deported to the Soviet interior between 1939 and 1941, printed in *Zeslancy Polscy w ZSSR* (Polish Nationals in the USSR). The Polish Embassy in Japan printed the book to help people contact loved ones released after August 12, 1941, seven weeks after German forces invaded the Soviet Union. *Alexander M. Schenker, Connecticut*

MAPA
ADMINISTRACYJNA
ZSRR

Map of the Soviet Union from *Zeslancy Polscy w ZSSR* (Polish Nationals in the USSR), which was used to identify the location of Polish citizens deported from Soviet-occupied territories between 1939 and 1941. *Alexander M. Schenker, Connecticut*

WE MUST DO NOTHING WHICH MIGHT PREVENT EXIT THESE VISA HOLDERS.[15]

At Beckelman's urging, the Joint ultimately spent $150,000 for refugee emigration from Lithuania.[16]

Most refugees found a way to purchase tickets with dollars. A handful of refugees managed to travel to Riga, Latvia, where the local Intourist office accepted rubles for the entire package.[17] But as Benjamin Fishoff recalled, this opportunity was short-lived. By the time he learned about the scheme, Intourist had forbidden the sale of tickets in Riga.[18]

SOVIET ULTIMATUM

In late fall 1940, ominous state actions brought renewed pressure on the refugees to leave the Soviet Union. In late November, Abraham Guzevicius, commissar for internal affairs for Soviet Lithuania, issued

an order to his division chiefs to prepare a list of all possibly unreliable elements in their jurisdictions:

> The index account must cover all those persons who by reason of their social and political past, national chauvinistic opinions, religious convictions, moral and political inconstance [*sic*], are opposed to the socialistic order and thus might be used by the intelligence services of foreign countries and by the counter-revolutionary cell for anti-soviet purposes.[19]

Those targeted included members of political parties considered anti-Soviet, former citizens of foreign countries, and members of religious organizations. The comprehensive list covered virtually every Jewish refugee in Vilna. Individuals struggling to emigrate legally were caught in the net, because the list included people "having personal correspondence and maintaining correspondence abroad, with foreign legations and consulates"—an almost daily practice of everyone desperate to escape the oppressions of Soviet Lithuania.[20]

From their experience in Soviet-occupied Poland, the refugees well knew that the Soviets might use such a list as the basis for mass deportations of Jews to Russia's interior. That fear became fact six months later. On June 14 and 15, 1941, some 30,000 people were moved by train from Lithuania deep into Soviet territory, among them between 6,000 and 12,000 local and refugee Jews.[21]

In early January 1941, ripples of panic swept through the refugee community when the Soviet government decreed that all refugees in its territories had until January 25, 1941, to accept Soviet citizenship or be declared permanently stateless. Although the Soviet decree did not explicitly state the consequences for those who refused citizenship, the implications were clear to many people. Urgent cable appeals to the Joint's New York office warned:

> RECEIVED ALARMING CABLES. . . . JANUARY
> 25TH IS LIMIT FOR SOVIET CITIZENSHIP OR
> BE REMOVED TO SIBERIA.[22]

The refugees reasoned that if they rejected Soviet citizenship, they would be deported to forced labor camps, but to accept meant that as Soviet nationals they, like the natives of the Baltic States who automatically became Soviet citizens at the time of occupation, would be forbidden to emigrate. If trapped in Soviet territory, they despaired of leading productive lives and of ever seeing relatives left behind in Poland, let alone being able to live freely as Jews.

When the Soviets issued their citizenship decree, about 12,000 Polish Jewish refugees were still living in Lithuania.[23] By the Joint's accounting, as many as 3,000 of them, including a group with certificates to Palestine, had destination visas.[24] Of those without any of the documents necessary to apply for Soviet exit permits, the Joint reported that "the great bulk" of them

would elect for Soviet citizenship.[25] The rest, who still hoped to flee, approached the task with renewed energy, fueled by desperation, for they assumed no exit permits would be issued after the January 25 deadline. With thousands of refugees holding destination visas and desperate to emigrate, Beckelman accurately assessed that their opportunity for flight was "now or never."[26]

Providing assistance, however, suddenly became an almost insurmountable challenge. In a cable of January 9, 1941, the Joint's Lisbon office reported:

> REFUGEE SECTION LIT[HUANIAN] RED CROSS
> INCLUDING ALL SUBSIDIARY REFUGEE AID
> COMMITTEES DISSOLVED MUST COMPLETE
> LIQUIDATION JANUARY 10TH.[27]

The Soviets had ordered the relief agencies closed. Beckelman faced the Herculean task of assisting hundreds of refugees within the space of weeks. Deprived of an office,

Suitcase label from the Hotel Novo Moscovskaya in Moscow, where many of the refugees stayed. *Dr. Norbert I. Swislocki, New York*

Red Square was one of the sites visited by refugees during their brief stopover in Moscow. *Anonymous*

Postcard of Moscow scene purchased by a refugee. *Dr. Mark Fishaut, New York*

FLIGHT AND RESCUE

he moved his operations to a hotel room. The hotel staff's objections to the crowds of refugees who gathered there caused him some consternation, but he refused to quit.[28] He continued to work for the refugees' benefit until leaving himself on February 21, 1941; like the refugees, he followed the route across the Soviet Union to Japan.

Just as Soviet authorities seemed to be putting up new blockades on the emigration process, they began to issue exit permits more liberally in January 1941, even to men of military age holding only Polish citizenship papers. Suddenly, the refugees' hopes were renewed. But at the same time, as Beckelman cabled the Joint,

The refugees with exit visas now found
themselves with only a matter of weeks in
which to secure dollars for passage or else
miss the chance to escape. Samuel Soltz,
who left in February 1941, wrote, "After
handing in my application to the NKVD,
the question of money gave me no peace.
I couldn't possibly save it up so fast. All
of us were in the same position."[30] Soltz
was among the few who paid for his train
ticket in rubles, but he had to sell his watch,
sheets, fountain pens, and extra shoes—
all but the barest necessities—in order to
obtain the cash before his permit expired.

The Soviets accepted exit applications until
February 10, 1941. The Joint estimated that
several thousand application permits were
pending when the Soviets stopped consider-
ing them.[31]

STOPOVER IN MOSCOW

After the refugees' long and arduous
struggle to find a way out of Lithuania, the
trip across the Soviet interior was some-
thing of an anticlimax. The trans-Siberian
train originated in Moscow, and they spent
anywhere from several hours to a few
days waiting for a rail connection. To their
amazement, they were treated as tourists
rather than refugees for the first time since
their odyssey began. Intourist ticket packages included accommodations in Moscow's
better hotels, sightseeing tours, and tickets
for museums and theaters. Many of the
refugees stayed at the Novo-Moscovskaya,
a hotel normally reserved for Russian
officers and diplomats, which provided
spacious, well-furnished rooms with private
baths. Foods that had been undreamed of
since the outbreak of war were available.
When the Mir Yeshiva students passed
through, they delighted in ordering oranges
in February—in the middle of the Russian
winter.[32]

- 3 - 1296, October 6, 2 p.m. from Moscow

cursory interrogation. However, as all of the members
of the groups that have thus far passed through Moscow were in possession of Japanese transit visas,
presumably the situation created by the brevity of
their stay in Moscow can be dealt with in Tokyo.

I assume the Department is aware of the fact that
Japanese transit visas were issued to these individuals on the basis of assurances made to the Japanese
Legation in Kaunas by the Dutch Consul at the instance
of the representative of the Joint Distribution
Committee in Kaunas that entrance visas to the Dutch
possessions in the Americas were not required and
that approximately 2,000 Japanese transit visas of
this type were recently issued in Kaunas, specifying
on the face of the visa that the applicants were en
route to the Dutch possessions in the Americas.
Each of the applicants thus far examined by the Embassy
in Moscow regarded his Japanese transit visa marked
as en route to the Dutch possessions in the Americas as
merely a means of obtaining a Soviet exit visa and
transit across Japan with the intention of entering
the United States and remaining there for at least the
duration of the war.

STEINHARDT

PEG

ABOVE: Cable sent October 6,
1940, by U.S. Ambassador
Laurence A. Steinhardt in
Moscow to alert Washington
that about 2,000 Japanese
transit visas had recently
been issued in Kaunas.
*National Archives and
Records Administration,
Washington, D.C.*

LEFT: Ambassador Steinhardt,
who interviewed some refugees during their stopover in
Moscow. *National Archives
and Records Administration,
College Park, Maryland*

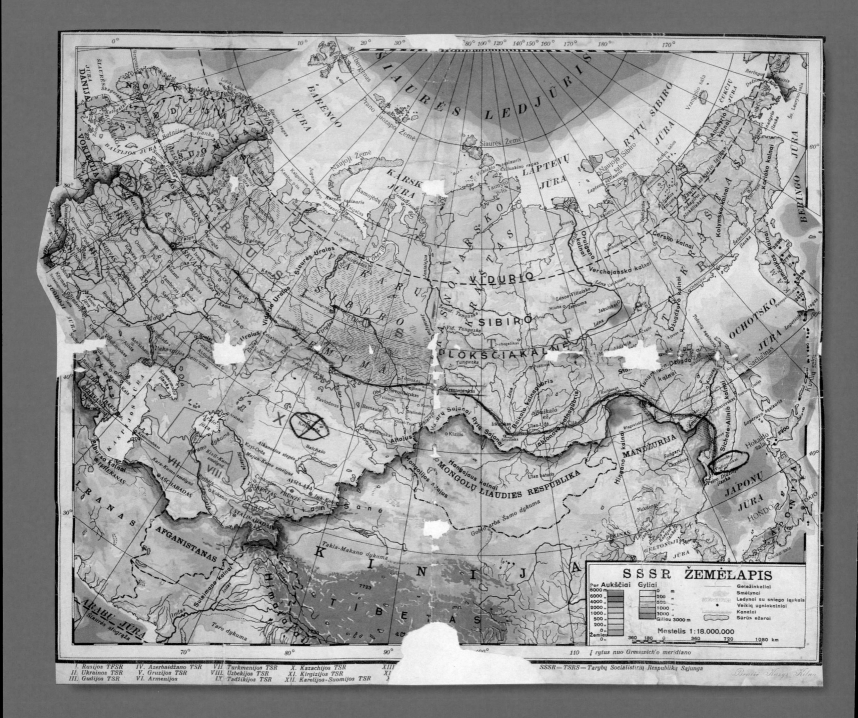

Map (with place names in Lithuanian) of the Sondheimer family's route across the Soviet Union to Vladivostok. The X over the city of Karaganda indicates the place to which the Soviets deported other family members. Several died there. *Hanni L. Vogelweid, California*

During their brief stay in Moscow, many refugees hoped to pick up U.S. visas at the American Embassy. Unfortunately, most could not schedule the required interview with Ambassador Laurence Steinhardt before their trains were to depart for Vladivostok. When Mendel Mozes was told he would have to wait ten or fifteen minutes to see the ambassador, he decided not to risk missing his train connection and abruptly left.[33] The refugees judged it preferable to leave Soviet territory and search for final destinations once they reached Japan. Certainly no one was going to return to Lithuania. Like the refugees, Steinhardt felt that since everyone he had met possessed a Japanese transit visa, "the situation created by the brevity" of people's stays in Moscow could "be dealt with in Tokyo."[34]

In one of Steinhardt's cables to the State Department in Washington reporting on the refugees' arrival in Moscow, the ambassador alerted his superiors to the apparent deceptive use of visas issued by the Dutch and Japanese consuls in Kaunas. On October 6, 1940, he wrote:

> Approximately 2,000 Japanese transit visas . . . were recently issued in Kaunas, specifying on the face of the visa that the applicants were en route to the Dutch possessions in the Americas. Each of the applicants thus far examined by the Embassy in Moscow regarded his Japanese transit visa marked as en route to the Dutch possessions in the Americas as merely a means of obtaining a Soviet exit visa and transit across Japan with the intention of entering the United States and remaining there for at least the duration of the war.[35]

In the same cable Steinhardt hinted that "the representative of the Joint Distribution Committee in Kaunas"—the unnamed Moses Beckelman—had played a role in the scheme by intervening on the refugees' behalf with the "Dutch Consul," who, in turn, provided "assurances" to the "Japanese Legation in Kaunas." This information,

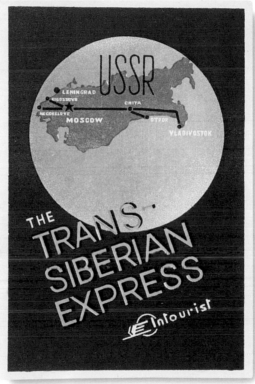

as well as the number of "approximately 2,000" Japanese transit visas, was probably given to Steinhardt by Beckelman in a meeting with the ambassador in Moscow in late September 1940.[36]

ACROSS SIBERIA

The 5,800-mile route of the Trans-Siberian Railroad, built during the reigns of Russia's last two tsars, connected the European

ABOVE: The Trans-Siberian Railroad traveled across many barren but beautiful stretches of land. *Corbis/Bettmann, New York*

RIGHT: The vast, desolate terrain near Chita, Siberia, was along the route of the Trans-Siberian Railroad. *National Archives and Records Administration, Washington, D.C.*

OPPOSITE: The "Joseph Stalin" diesel locomotive was the type most commonly used on the Trans-Siberian Railroad from the mid-1930s to the mid-1940s. *David King Collection, London*

Posters printed in 1929 promoted the sale of lottery tickets to fund Jewish settlement in the east Siberian region of Birobidzhan. A brief stopover there en route to Vladivostok led some of the refugees to conclude that Soviet policies offered little hope for a thriving Jewish community in the area. *The Mitchell Wolfson Jr. Collection, The Wolfsonian—Florida International University, Miami Beach*

ABOVE: Vladivostok, the eastern terminus for the Trans-Siberian Railroad. *National Archives and Records Administration, Washington, D.C.*

RIGHT: U.S. $20 gold coins smuggled out of the USSR in the lining of a refugee's suitcase. *Dr. Mark Fishaut, New York*

FAR RIGHT: Receipt for rubles confiscated by Soviet authorities in Vladivostok. *Rabbi Moshe Zupnik, New York*

continent to the Pacific Ocean and required a travel time of nine or ten days. In the less expensive "hard class," travelers rode on wooden benches; those who could afford "soft class" were provided with amenities that rivaled first-class travel in western Europe. Wanda Glass and her husband, having sold a 13-karat diamond ring to purchase their train tickets, found the accommodations to be luxurious and the dining service excellent.[37] Hanni Sondheimer Vogelweid remembered eating "lots of caviar" and wonderful cakes in the train's elegant dining car. After selling most of their possessions for rubles, which could not be taken out of Soviet territory, the Sondheimers spent their cash freely during the trans-Siberian journey.[38]

Most refugees, however, had barely managed to scrape together the funds for passage and therefore traveled "hard class." Accommodations were simple but adequate. Included in the price of the Intourist ticket were bread, herring, sugar, and hot water for tea. Most of the refugees brought food

of their own or purchased what they could from vendors at stations along the way. Those who observed kosher dietary laws usually packed dry cheese or sausage for the trip.[39] The railroad issued bedding, although the "mattresses" were worn so thin that they seemed like little more than blankets. Still, the passengers were thankful that at least their compartments remained warm as the train traveled across the wintry landscape.

Even the comfort of the cars and the train's rhythmic swaying were not enough to calm the fears of some émigrés. The conductors' frequent inspections were an ordeal for the travelers, many of whom feared that their papers would not hold up under scrutiny. They were probably wise to remain wary. From Japan, Poland's Ambassador Romer reported:

Until they had left Vladivostok, the travelers were never sure of being able to leave the U.S.S.R. In fact there have been cases in which persons, sometimes whole

The *Amakusa Maru,* one of the ships that took the refugees from Vladivostok across the Sea of Japan to the Japanese port city of Tsuruga. *City of Tsuruga, Recollections of Hometown Tsuruga (Tsuruga, 1987)*

96

port of Tsuruga were tossed about in the stormy waters like toy boats, consigning passengers to seasickness and misery. Berthed in the ships' overloaded holds, some of the refugees despaired of reaching Japan safely.[48] The trip, which took 36 hours in calm waters, could stretch to 60 hours in stormy weather. A ship carrying many of the Mir Yeshiva students to Japan listed so sharply at times that the passengers were unable to get up from the floor.[49]

Despite privations, fear, and seasickness, the refugees were united in rejoicing, singing, and dancing when they finally left Soviet waters.[50] The NKVD usually accompanied the small steamers out of Soviet territory. As these escorts headed back to land, the refugees breathed a collective sigh of relief. Oskar Schenker later wrote:

> As we crossed the sea towards Japan, we waited in quiet anxiety for the day when we should pass beyond Russian territorial waters. It came at last, the Red flag was lowered and the Soviet officials left the ship. Freedom lay ahead. Japan was to be for us really the land of the rising sun.[51]

The exit from the Soviet Union peaked during January and February 1941, when more than 1,300 people arrived in Japan from the USSR.[52] After March, the numbers greatly dwindled, but people trickled out of Vladivostok and crossed the Sea of Japan right up to June 1941 and the German invasion of the Soviet Union.[53]

OPPOSITE: Japanese shipping company poster, 1934, proclaims: "The Sea Is Our Destiny." *Yokohama Maritime Museum*

6 STRANDED

ARRIVING IN JAPAN

When the Jewish refugees left Poland in the fall of 1939, they had no idea they were embarking on an odyssey that would take them halfway around the world. Arriving in Japan, "staggering with exhaustion," in the words of one émigré, many were nearly penniless.[1] The Szepsenwol sisters, for example, landed in Japan sharing one dress, a skirt and blouse, and carrying their few other belongings in a small woven basket.[2] In contrast to the approximately 2,000 Jews from Germany and Austria who reached Japan after January 1940 and quickly moved on, the 2,178 Polish Jewish refugees who arrived between July 1940 and August 1941 were "in the main completely destitute and lacking documents to enable them to proceed further."[3]

When the Polish Jews arrived in Japan, they found a small community of Jews of eastern European origins, who felt a natural kinship with them. Prosperous and relatively secure, this group of about 25 Ashkenazi families, most of whom had been driven from Russia by the 1917 revolution, resided in the large port city of Kobe and enjoyed good relations with their Japanese neighbors and the authorities. One of their respected leaders, Anatole Ponevejsky, mobilized the Kobe Jewish community and formed the Committee for Assistance to Refugees. Ponevejsky, whose family had settled in Kobe in the mid-1930s, had led

THE OSAKA MAINICHI &

More Hebrews Arrive In 'Nippon

Approximately 340 Jews driven from Europe came to Nippon by the Japan Sea liner Amakusa Maru, entering Tsuruga on Thursday afternoon, February 13.

340 Jews Relieved To Reach Tsuruga; Tragedy-Etched Faces Smile With Joy

— *Amakusa Maru Brings Refugees Fleeing Europe* —

TSURUGA, Feb. 13.—Tragedy-etched faces smiled with joyful relief and reassurance today, as the liner Amakusa Maru came through a [...] languages spoken, and in stark, poverty-stricken tragedy.

Jewish couples, torn from all that they ever held dear, possessed of onl[...]

OPPOSITE: Jewish refugees in Kobe, Japan, April 1941. Photograph by Toru Kono. *Private Collection, courtesy of Osaka City Museum of Modern Art*

LEFT: *Osaka Mainichi & Tokyo Nichi Nichi*, February 15, 1941.

an earlier effort to organize local Jews to build a community center, synagogue, and kosher butcher shop. As the director of his family's export-import business, Ponevejsky was the natural choice to be president of the new committee, popularly known by its cable address, Jewcom.

Alex Triguboff and other representatives of Jewcom greeted the steamers carrying refugees from Vladivostok at the port of Tsuruga on Japan's west coast. To the refugees' great relief, the Jewcom agents

זה השער לה צדיקים יבאו בו

DRAWING BY A. TAUB

„JEWCOM"
KOBE

JEWISH COMMUNITY (ASHKENAZIM)
KOBE • 1941 • JAPAN

ABOVE: Kobe Jewish Community Center, 1941. *Private Collection, courtesy of Osaka City Museum of Modern Art*

LEFT: Cover for report on assistance to refugees drawn by A. Taub, a refugee. Jewcom was the cable address for the small Jewish community in Kobe. *Mrs. Keiko Triguboff, California*

OPPOSITE, TOP: Four members of the Jewcom Ladies' Committee in Kobe distribute clothing to the refugees. *USHMM, Gift of Irene Borevitz and Tamara Rozanski*

OPPOSITE, BOTTOM: Leaders of the Jewish community in Kobe, including Anatole Ponevejsky (standing in back, third from left), and members of the American Jewish Joint Distribution Committee and other relief agencies meet with refugees in Kobe, 1941. *USHMM, Gift of Irene Borevitz and Tamara Rozanski*

attended to all landing formalities. "Having earned the trust and confidence of the Japanese harbor police," wrote the committee's vice-president, Moise Moiseeff, "Jewcom exercise[d] all the prerogatives of a Consul" and ensured that all papers were in order and that entry into Japan could proceed.[4] With landing formalities completed, the travelers gathered their few belongings and headed to the train station for the 100-mile ride south to Kobe.

On board the train, the refugees got their first view of Japan. "We kept looking out of the window and couldn't get over the beauty of both the natural and man-made scenery and the use of space," Samuel Soltz recalled.[5] Equally dramatic was Kobe's sea-side setting. Lying along Osaka Bay, the city was surrounded by a ridge of mountains.

Once in Kobe, the refugees looked to Jewcom as their main provider. Ponevejsky directed a staff of eight men whose most important task was mediating between the refugees and the authorities. The wives attended to material

Anatole Ponevejsky
(1900–1969)

Anatole Ponevejsky was born in Irkutsk, Siberia. Educated at the university in Irkutsk, he moved with his brothers, Leo and David, to Harbin, Manchuria, in about 1930, where they established the firm Ponevejsky Brothers—importers of woolen goods. The business grew quickly, and in 1935 Anatole and his wife, Gita, moved to Yokohama, Japan. Three years later, they went to Kobe.

Ponevejsky's colleagues from Kobe remembered him as "a very fine man," cheerful and optimistic. Behind the pleasant demeanor was a shrewd and persuasive business-man who was equally at ease meeting with Japanese military authorities, discussing points of Judaic law with the luminaries of Jewish scholarship who passed through Japan, or playing with his two young daughters.

Ill health forced Ponevejsky to step down from the presidency of Jewcom in 1941. He traveled to the United States for treatment in May. Although Ponevejsky was thousands of miles from Kobe, his colleagues at Jewcom continued to look to him for leadership, sending him monthly reports until the Jewcom office finally closed in October 1941.

After the war, Ponevejsky returned to Japan and opened a retail store in Tokyo, where he employed for a brief time the former consul, Chiune Sugihara.

PHOTO: *USHMM, Gift of Irene Borevitz and Tamara Rozanski*

needs, organizing the distribution of the committee's relief funds, overseeing the hostels where most of the refugees lived, and comforting the elderly and ailing. In the words of one observer, "If one considers that this enormous work has been carried out by a Community consisting of slightly over twenty families one can't help admiring the extent of their work, as well as the way all these people have given up their businesses, their private life, and have taken to this exhausting relief work."[6]

At first, Jewcom's members donated their own money for refugee support, but when the trickle of people into Japan became a

flood, they turned to the Joint Distribution Committee for help. The Joint provided most of the $350,000 for the refugees' lodging, food, and emigration expenses in 1940 and 1941.[7] Supplemental monies came from Vaad ha-Hatzala and Agudath Israel in the United States, HICEM in Europe, and the embassy of the Polish government-in-exile in Tokyo.

Sufficiently if not amply provided for, Jewcom allocated 1.50 yen (about 25 cents) daily to each refugee, a sum later reduced as the Joint's resources were spread thin. The refugees used this stipend to purchase fish, vegetables, and fruit in local markets.

Tourist guidebook for Kobe, with cover photograph of a statue of the 14th-century general Kusunoki Masahige at the Minatogawa Shrine.
Dr. Mark Fishaut, New York

Each day Jewcom distributed bread from its offices. Even after Japan instituted food rationing in April 1941, the refugees, who were unaccustomed to a rice-based diet, were allowed a large allotment of flour.[8] Jewcom also operated hostels for needy refugees. By March 1941, more than a thousand refugees were living in 23 group homes located in the less expensive suburbs of Kobe, a short train ride from Jewcom headquarters on Yamamoto-Dori Street. Susan Bluman recalled sharing a house with nearly 30 other refugees, sleeping ten or 12 people in each room.[9]

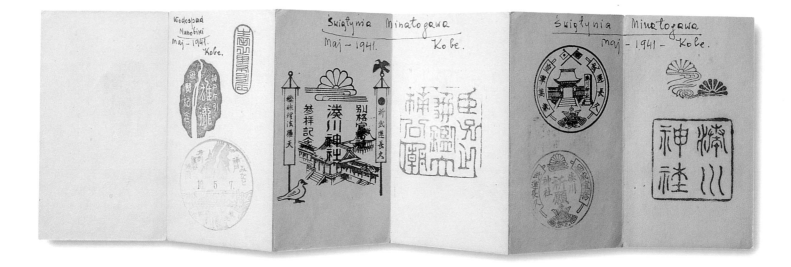

"THE OTHER": JEWISH-JAPANESE ENCOUNTERS

With their material needs taken care of, some refugees found time to visit places of interest.[10] Japan's sites and attractions offered a brief distraction from the on-going worries about final destinations and loved ones still in Poland. "The stunning change of scenery—physical, human and spiritual—aroused our curiosity," wrote Zorach Warhaftig, who arrived in Japan in the fall of 1940.[11] Transportation was cheap, museums were free, and nearby parks and waterfalls beckoned. Ruth Lax paid for a hotel and sightseeing in Kyoto with a refund of her unused Intourist coupons. When she first demanded repayment at the Soviet consulate, the diplomats there laughed at her. She threatened to write to major news-papers denouncing Intourist, and the diplo-mats quickly relented and gave her the full value of the coupons in yen.[12]

During their stay, the refugees were touched by the kindness of the Japanese, who regarded them with curiosity. About one-quarter of the refugees were yeshiva students and rabbis who maintained their prescribed study schedule. Chanting their prayers audibly in the quiet Kobe evenings, they attracted inquisitive stares. The refugees as a whole captured the interest of a group of avant-garde photog-raphers, who took pictures of many of them in late March 1941. That May the members of the Tanpei Photography Club displayed 22 of their works in an exhibition in Osaka titled *Wandering Jew*. Kaneyoshi Tabuchi wrote about his sensitive portrait of a yeshiva student: "What is floating in the wanderer's brow is not only sorrow and misery . . . but also the tenacity of a people gloomily scattered throughout the world."[13]

The local Japanese became accustomed to the refugees, extending generous hospi-tality. If the Jewcom doctor or nurse was unable to diagnose or treat a malady, the refugee patient was referred to Japanese specialists, often at no cost. Jewcom's secre-tary, Leo Hanin, recalled, "When one of the children became very sick and when the Japanese doctor who was called to treat him took him to his private hospital, the doctor refused to accept any money for his services and the hospital when he found out the child was a refugee."[14] Also, according to Hanin, local farmers contacted Jewcom to say they would be honored to give the chil-dren gifts of fruit they had grown. "They came the next week with boxes and boxes of fresh, beautiful apples and oranges and personally presented each child with some of the fruits. They were humble, decent, good people."[15]

WANDERING JEW

AN EXHIBITION BY THE

TANPEI PHOTOGRAPHY CLUB

OSAKA, JAPAN, MAY 1941

Mother by Nakaji Yasui. *On deposit at the Hyogo Prefectural Museum of Modern Art, Kobe*

Child by Nakaji Yasui. *Ms. Hinoshita, Japan*

Man by Kaneyoshi Tabuchi. *Mrs. Kiyoko Tabuchi, Collection of the Tokyo Metropolitan Museum of Photography*

Window by Nakaji Yasui. *On deposit at the Hyogo Prefectural Museum of Modern Art, Kobe*

Nap by Osamu Shiihara. *Mr. Tomatsu Shiihara, on deposit at the Hyogo Prefectural Museum of Modern Art, Kobe*

Friends by Osamu Shiihara. *Mr. Tomatsu Shiihara, on deposit at the Hyogo Prefectural Museum of Modern Art, Kobe*

Profile by Nakaji Yasui. *On deposit at the Hyogo Prefectural Museum of Modern Art, Kobe*

Fugitives D by Osamu Shiihara. *Mr. Tomatsu Shiihara, Gift to the National Museum of Modern Art, Tokyo*

Untitled by Toru Kono. *Private Collection, courtesy of the Osaka City Museum of Modern Art*

Hebrew Book by Osamu Shiihara. *Mr. Tomatsu Shiihara, on deposit at the Hyogo Prefectural Museum of Modern Art, Kobe*

Untitled by Toru Kono. *Private Collection, courtesy of the Osaka City Museum of Modern Art*

Luggage by Toru Kono. *Mr. Keizo Kono, Collection of the Tokyo Metropolitan Museum of Photography*

Father and Child by Kaneyoshi Tabuchi. *Mrs. Kiyoko Tabuchi, Collection of the Tokyo Metropolitan Museum of Photography*

Chess by Kaneyoshi Tabuchi. *Mrs. Kiyoko Tabuchi, Japan*

ABOVE: Members of a Polish Jewish writers' group, including Yiddish actress Rose Shoshana Kahan (center, wearing necklace), observe Passover in Kobe, 1941. *Joseph Fiszman, Oregon*

CENTER: Photograph of Abus and Sara Arnfeld, sent from Warsaw by Sara to her husband, Chaim, in Kobe, c.1941. *USHMM, Gift of Leo Arnfeld*

RIGHT: Receipt for a parcel sent by Markus Nowogrodzki to his mother in the Warsaw ghetto. Packages of tea and other items from Japan could be sold or traded on the black market by relatives trapped in occupied Poland. *Markus Nowogrodzki, New York*

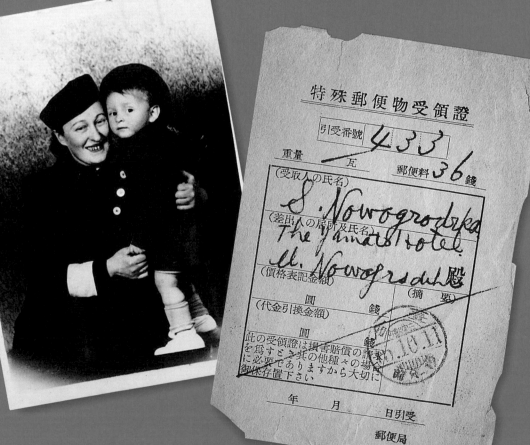

FAMILIES LEFT BEHIND

Despite the kind reception and the interesting sites to visit, families and friends left behind were constantly in the refugees' thoughts. People would gather daily at Jewcom's offices, searching the bulletin board for news. Rose Shoshana Kahan described the scene:

> As always I went to the committee office to meet acquaintances, to read the lists of (arrived) letters. . . . Perhaps there is a letter. . . . One walks around as shadows by the walls of the committee office, one waits with impatience for the "list," which the committee hangs every day on the wall of the gate, with names of those who received letters or telegrams.[16]

Correspondence might bring news about future prospects, affidavits of support, money for ship tickets, or word from friends and relatives in Europe. Jews still in Lithuania bombarded the refugee-aid organizations in Japan with cables seeking help to obtain visas.

Thousands of miles from home, every refugee worried about family members trapped in German- and Soviet-occupied territories. For Passover in April 1941, Jewcom imported matzahs for the refugees, enabling them to put together a traditional Seder. The occasion triggered in Rose Shoshana Kahan strong emotions of joy, sadness, and guilt about her two grown children left behind:

Postcards sent to the refugees in Kobe, care of Jewcom, from relatives still in Nazi- and Soviet-occupied territory. Rabbi Moshe Zupnik, New York; USHMM, Gifts of Syma Crane and Bella Herson

PAMIĄTKA Z KRYNICY

In 1941 Jacob Fiszman and his son, Josef, purchased pearls in Kobe, intending to give them to his wife and daughter when they were reunited. The photograph shows the family together before the war. In 1941 Gale (standing) and Ursula Fiszman were living in the Warsaw ghetto; two years later they were deported to a Nazi death camp. *Rachele Noto Fiszman and Joseph Fiszman, Oregon*

Such a beautiful table with such fine food. The mouth is watering, the palate is stimulated, the eyes get larger, one waits impatiently to grab a piece of gefilte fish, which smiles to you from the plate. . . . One starts to sit down at the table. Suddenly all are sad. Why do we deserve such a meal? Our most beloved and closest to us languish in prisons, in the ghettos. . . . Why are we the chosen? Why do we get fish and meat? While they don't even have a small piece of bread?[17]

"It was our duty to come to the aid of our relatives and friends," Zorach Warhaftig recalled. "Some of my friends economized on their own meals so as to be able to send provisions to their kinfolk."[18] The people back home could barter a small package of Japanese tea for an entire week's worth of food.[19] From Japan, Chaim Arnfeld regularly mailed home to Warsaw packages of provisions, and the letters from his wife, Sara, revealed the pain of separation:

As for me, I work and life goes on. . . . Everybody is together, too bad you are missing. . . . Try to stay well so you can live in the future for your beloved son. . . . I know that you will be crying when you see [photographs of him], but what can we do, we have to be strong and survive all that. . . . Believe me there are days when I just want to cry because I truly need you and miss you.[20]

Further correspondence with occupied Poland was for the most part abruptly halted by Operation Barbarossa, Germany's invasion of the USSR on June 22, 1941. By the end of 1941, most Jews in German-occupied Poland had been forced to live in ghettos, and hundreds died daily from starvation, disease, and exhaustion from forced labor. By 1942, the Germans had initiated the systematic deportation of Polish Jews from the ghettos to Auschwitz-Birkenau, Treblinka, and other killing centers equipped with gas chambers. Jewish refugees like Chaim Arnfeld, who reached Japan in early 1941, learned about the fates of their families only in late 1945, at war's end.

What was the fate of Polish Jewish refugees who did not seek to escape from Lithuania? A minority, including several hundred yeshiva students, survived the war in the Soviet interior, where they had been sent in mass deportations carried out shortly before the German invasion.[21] The majority of those who remained in Vilna, Kaunas, or small towns in the countryside did not survive the Nazi genocide. In Lithuania and then elsewhere in Soviet territory captured by German forces, the organized mass murder of Jews began in the summer of 1941 with large-scale shootings by the Germans and their collaborators. Mobile killing squads, the *Einsatzgruppen,* were attached to German army units and deployed behind the front lines to conduct their murderous operations. In July 1941, the *Einsatzgruppen* and their collaborators killed approximately 5,000 Jews in Vilna, while the surviving Jews of Kaunas were ordered into a ghetto.

A column of Jews in a pit in Ponary, a killing site six miles outside of Vilna, await execution, late June–July 1941. Here the Nazis and their Lithuanian collaborators executed some 35,000 Jews before the Vilna ghetto was sealed on September 6, 1941. *YIVO Institute for Jewish Research, New York*

Some of the refugees still in Lithuania had received visas from Zwartendijk and Sugihara but for various reasons never used them. Israel Friedmann (no. 2,096 on Sugihara's list of visa recipients) was arrested on September 23, 1941, imprisoned in Vilna's Lukishki Prison, and shot on October 4, 1941, at Ponary, an *Einsatzgruppen* killing site in a wooded area outside the city.[22] Irena Dwinson (no. 566 on Sugihara's list), who survived as a child hidden with an uncle in Ukraine, learned after the war that her parents, Sara and Benjamin Dwinson (nos. 567 and 568), were killed by Germans in the Lida area, and her uncle, Aron Wekeler (no. 565), was murdered by Lithuanian collaborators near Vilna.[23]

JAPANESE AUTHORITIES AND JEWISH REFUGEES

The early 1941 flood of Jewish refugees caused some consternation among Japanese higher authorities, who could not foresee the events that would end the flow. At the local level, however, the presence of Jewcom agents assuaged port authorities in Tsuruga: "Our Community has come to an understanding with the Tsuruga and local Police Authorities as to letting the groups pass without any difficulties under the personal guarantee of our Community."[24] Refugees with incomplete or invalid visas were released to Jewcom's care, a status marked in the transients' identity papers. Abe Brumberg received a typical notation:

> Although the applicant does not have visas to enter the destination countries, (s)he has the cash necessary to land on Japan and reservations for a boarding pass, and (s)he intends to follow the procedure to obtain visas for the destination countries in Tokyo during the transit period, and therefore (s)he was admitted based on the guarantee by the Kobe Jewish Association.[25]

For refugees with valid destination visas but no money, the stamps read:

> Although the applicant has entry visas, (s)he does not have any money and cannot leave Japan within the transit period, and therefore, (s)he was admitted based on the guarantee of the Kobe Jewish Association.[26]

Jewcom gave Japanese authorities two guarantees: it would finance the refugees' stay in Japan, and it would make every effort to ensure their departure to other countries. The committee's staff honored the first part of the agreement but had less success with the second despite valiant efforts. By February 1941, more than a thousand refugees were under the care of Jewcom. The following month the number stranded in Japan grew to 1,724.[27] As Ponevejsky observed, even after obtaining new destination visas, it often took four or five months to make all the arrangements for departure.[28]

The refugees' transit visas were initially valid for seven to 15 days. To their immense relief, because they had nowhere to go, the authorities of the Hyogo Prefecture (where Kobe was located) issued renewable "Permits to Stay in Japan," which extended the transit period for up to two months. Most refugees stayed in Japan far longer than two weeks; more than a third of them remained for at least eight months.[29] Some children even resumed their education: Lejb Melamdowicz went to an international primary school in Kobe, and Hanni Sondheimer learned stenography in Yokohama.

The mounting number of refugees and the growing likelihood of war in the Pacific caused Japanese authorities to become increasingly concerned. The *Kempeitai* (military police organization) was especially uneasy because Kobe was a major military depot. Although *Kempeitai* agents, suspicious of all foreigners, kept close tabs on the newcomers' movements, the Japanese treated Jews no differently than they did other westerners, in keeping with the spirit of the Five Ministers Conference of December 1938.

A striking episode in February 1941 underscored Japan's continuing adherence to its distinctive policy toward Jews. As reported by Jewcom's secretary, Leo Hanin, "Representatives of the Dept. of Military Affairs requested that Jewcom send to Tokyo three representatives of the Jewish refugees."[30] Jewcom selected three rabbis to accompany Hanin on the trip. The four men were filled with trepidation when they were met by the Japanese delegation: two generals and two admirals in full dress uniforms, swords on the table in front of them, and several Shinto priests in brightly colored robes. One general asked bluntly why the Germans hated the Jews. Rabbi Shimon Kalisch, himself a refugee, answered, "The Germans hate everyone who is not blond and blue-eyed, and besides they hate the Jews because we are Asiatic people like you, the Japanese."[31] Kalisch's answer apparently satisfied the generals,

who instructed the men to return to Kobe and not worry.

In an effort to understand the source and extent of the refugee problem, the Japanese Foreign Ministry cabled Sugihara in February 1941 and all its other consuls in Europe in March, asking how many visas had been

ABOVE: Crayon case given to Lejb Melamdowicz, who was briefly enrolled in a school in Japan. *Leo Melamed, Illinois*

LEFT: Lacking final destination visas, most of the Polish Jewish refugees stayed in Japan long after their 10-day transit visas had expired. Many feared that Japanese authorities would refuse to extend their stay with permits like this one. *Ruth Berkowicz Segal, New Hampshire*

A group of rabbis attend a meeting with Japanese military and religious leaders at the naval headquarters in Kobe in the spring of 1941. From left to right: Rabbi Shlomo Shapiro, Professor Setsuzo Kotsuji, Rabbi Szymon Kalisch, Rabbi Moses Shatzkes, Captain Yuzuru Fukamachi, and Jewcom representative Leo Hanin. *YIVO Institute for Jewish Research, New York*

issued and under what circumstances.[32] With all the data in hand, in April 1941 the Foreign Ministry reported its findings about why refugees with transit visas were becoming stranded in Japan. First, a number of countries had tightened their requirements after issuing destination visas. "In addition to entry visas issued by their consulates," the report stated, these nations "now require entry permits from their respective governments." Second, the report specifically cited 2,132 visas granted by Sugihara and concluded—without mentioning the consul by name—that much of the problem was "largely due to the way the Kaunas Consulate issued visas."[33]

After learning that Sugihara had issued many transit visas in the absence of valid destination visas, Tokyo issued a directive

on March 19 to its embassy in Moscow and its consulate in Vladivostok. Diplomats were instructed to closely examine the validity of the refugees' destination visas and certify only those that passed this strict inspection with "a seal affixed on their visas. Those without such a seal may not board a Japanese vessel."[34] In response, the Japanese ambassador in Moscow cabled the Foreign Ministry that refugees already en route would have no knowledge of Tokyo's new regulations.[35] Unaware of the change in procedure, they were continuing across the Soviet Union to Vladivostok, where they expected to board ships for Japan.

The timing of Japan's new restrictions could not have been worse for the hopeful émigrés aboard the steamer *Amakusa Maru,* which departed Vladivostok in mid-March

1941. When the ship reached Tsuruga, harbor police found that 70 or 80 of the passengers had Japanese transit visas signed by Sugihara, but no destination visas. Before the March 19 directive, Jewcom's assurances would have gained entry for the refugees. Now, however, they were stopped. One of the passengers, Benjamin Fishoff, recalled what a crushing blow it was to be denied entry.

> We were soon back on the ship, and on the way back to Vladivostok. One can easily imagine our bitter hearts. It wasn't just the fact that we had to travel on the small ship again. We were afraid that this time the Russians would send us to Siberia as spies.[36]

In Vladivostok, Soviet authorities forbade the passengers to disembark. Huddled in the ship's hold, the refugees contemplated the worst. Suddenly the engines sprang to life. They were on their way back to Japan! "When we arrived in Japan the second time," said Fishoff, "a tremendous surprise awaited us." Through the intervention of Dutch diplomats in Kobe and Tokyo, Jewcom had managed to secure "Curaçao visas."[37] Playing out the charade—by this time Japanese authorities knew the "Curaçao visas" were useless—the Tsuruga harbor police admitted the refugees after receiving the usual assurances from Jewcom.

In actuality, it was Soviet pressure and not the Dutch intercession that reversed the fate of the passengers aboard the *Amakusa Maru*. G. N. Zarubin, a Soviet consular chief, met with the secretary of the Japanese Embassy in Moscow to discuss Japan's March 19 directive on visa recertification. The new regulations, Zarubin pointed out, had stranded in Vladivostok refugees holding Japanese transit visas. "Since we were not informed in time about the annulment by the Japanese authorities of visas that had already been issued," Zarubin told the secretary, "we categorically insist that all emigrants in Vladivostok who have visas issued by a Japanese consul be transported to Japan on the next available vessel."[38]

In Vladivostok, Japanese consul Saburo Nei bore the brunt of the Soviet position. Taking pity on the refugees, Nei, according to a Soviet Foreign Ministry recounting of events, disregarded standing orders from Tokyo and issued new visas to the blocked refugees. Nei's decision was both humanitarian and practical, based on his attempt to avoid conflict in Vladivostok and to keep the port open to Japanese vessels.[39] The upshot was the release of the *Amakusa Maru* passengers plus another 100 hapless refugees who had been blocked in Vladivostok.[40]

"Status Report of European Refugees Arriving in Japan," April 15, 1941, compiled by the Japanese Foreign Ministry to determine the reasons for the influx of refugees. *Japanese Foreign Ministry Diplomatic Record Office, Tokyo*

日本郵船經營太平洋航路圖

TOP: Menus from the *Tatuta Maru*, kept by Oscar Schenker as mementos of his voyage from Japan to the United States. Schenker and his brother, Alfred, arrived in the United States in 1941, where they spent much of their time trying to arrange for their wives, children, and mother to leave the Soviet Union. *Alexander M. Schenker, Connecticut*

ABOVE LEFT: Botanical souvenir of Japan. *Alexander M. Schenker, Connecticut*

ABOVE RIGHT: Map of the route to the United States taken by the *Tatuta Maru*. *Alexander M. Schenker, Connecticut*

IN REPLY REFER TO
FILE NO. 811.11-MELAMDOWICZ
DT/blc

THE FOREIGN SERVICE
OF THE
UNITED STATES OF AMERICA

DEPARTMENT OF STATE

AMERICAN CONSULATE GENERAL

Tokyo, March 27, 1941.

Special Delivery

Mr. Icchok Melamdowicz,
      Dai-iti Hotel,
            Tokyo.

Sir:

      The Consulate General refers to your call at
this office on March 12, 1941, regarding the applications of yourself, your wife and your son for
temporary visitor visas for the United States.

      I am glad to inform you that word has now been
received from the Department of State that the names
of your wife, Fejgla MELAMDOWICZ, and of your son,
Lejb MELANDOWICZ, can now be included in the list of
persons whose cases are sponsored by the American
Federation of Labor.

      You are requested to present yourselves with your
travel documents at this office at 2.00 p.m., on
Friday, March 28, 1941, to begin your formal applications for visas.

            Very truly yours,

            S. G. Slavens,
            American Consul.

M.S. TATUTA MARU, N.Y.K. LINE
日本郵船株式會社　龍田丸

RENEWED SEARCH FOR VISAS

While in Japan, the refugees' main task was to secure valid visas to other destinations. Between July 1940 and November 1941, more than 500 of the refugees from Poland managed to sail for the United States; another

700 traveled to other destinations, including Palestine, Canada, South and Central America, Australia, and New Zealand.[41]

"A refugee is pleased to be the proud possessor of a visa to Curaçao, happy to obtain an entry permit to whatever country will

TOP LEFT: Letter from the U.S. consul in Tokyo, March 27, 1941, informs Icchok Melamdowicz that, like him, his wife and son would receive immigration visas under the American Federation of Labor's sponsorship. They were among the last refugees to obtain such visas in Japan. *Leo Melamed, Illinois*

TOP RIGHT: Among the passengers aboard the *Asama Maru* en route to Canada, spring 1941, were (front row, left to right) Razla and Zelik Honigberg and Paulina (Honigberg) Fishaut; (back row, far left and far right) Bronislaw Honigberg and Salomon Fishaut. *Dr. Mark Fishaut, New York*

BOTTOM: Postcard of the *Tatuta Maru,* one of many NYK Line ships that transported refugees from Japan to destinations in the Americas and the British dominions. *Family of Rabbi David and Zipporah Lifshitz, New York*

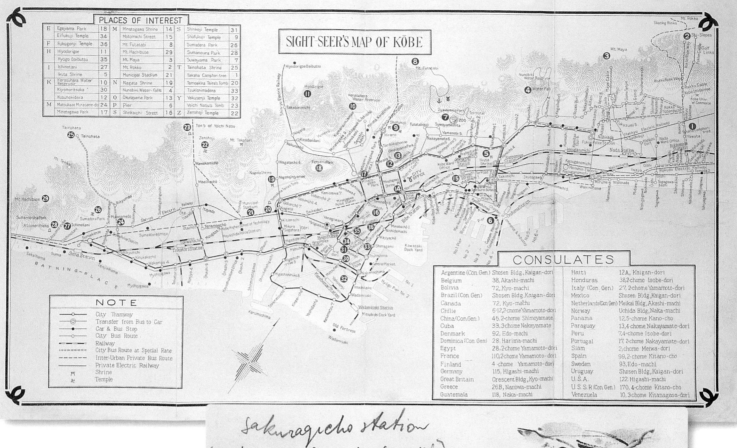

ABOVE: Jewish writer Abraham Swislocki used this map to locate consulates and other addresses in Kobe in 1941.
Dr. Norbert I. Swislocki, New York

RIGHT: In his efforts to obtain visas for his own family and other Jewish refugees, Zorach Warhaftig recorded on this postcard the addresses of embassies and consulates in Kobe, Tokyo, and Yokohama.
Yad Vashem Archives, Jerusalem

accept him—but his dreams are all of the United States. That is where he actually yearns to emigrate," wrote Moise Moiseeff in 1941.[42] But securing a U.S. visa often entailed a long, frustrating, and sometimes fruitless process. Although the United States had an embassy in Tokyo and consulates in Yokohama, Kobe, and Osaka, the majority of refugees applied to the consulate in Kobe, where they were living.

The decision to issue or withhold visas fell to the consuls in the field, who acted in accordance with instructions from the State Department. In the consulate building in Kobe, Vice Consul Roy Melbourne spent each morning interviewing the seemingly endless stream of people who crowded the corridors. He recalled that a representative of HICEM usually accompanied the applicants, testifying on their behalf.[43]

Melbourne's recommendations were accepted or rejected by his superior, Acting Consul Samuel Sokobin. HICEM's director in Kobe, J. Epstein, saw Sokobin as a roadblock: "Our very first interview with [Sokobin] gave us an idea of what our people could expect from his office. He was a definite anti-immigrationist. . . . He made a point of convincing us that it would be a misfortune for the refugees to proceed to the United States."[44]

On June 5, 1941, the State Department sent a circular telegram to its embassies and consulates with instructions to withhold U.S. visas from applicants with "children, parents, husband, wife, brothers or sisters still in controlled territory."[45] The cable warned that Germany and the USSR were likely to force refugees to act as intelligence agents in the United States by threatening reprisals against family members left behind. Moritz Sondheimer, learning that his relatives in the United States had sent affidavits of financial support for him and

his family, applied for a U.S. visa in Yokohama. When the officer asked if any relatives remained in occupied territories, he replied, "Yes, my mother." The visa was denied three days later.[46] Moise Moiseeff reported that the Kobe consular staff also was applying the State Department's new directive. "All the foundation work laid down by the Jewish organizations in the United States, all the 'Recommendations' and affidavits are now useless," he wrote.[47]

The Bloom–Van Nuys Act dealt another blow to the émigrés. Also designed to raise a barrier against infiltrators and fifth columnists, the law diminished overseas consuls' discretionary authority to issue visas and consolidated such control in State Department offices in Washington. As of July 1, when the law went into effect, refugees who were in the process of applying for U.S. visas not only had to begin anew but were now less likely to succeed. Jechel Lewin of Jewcom reported that "relatives in the USA [were compelled] to

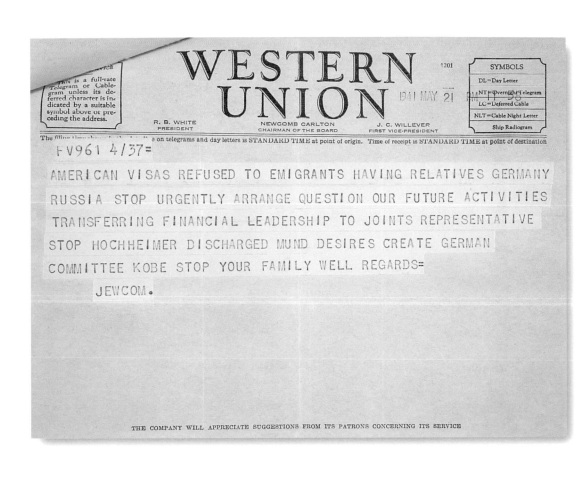

apply first to the State Dept. in Washington and only if and after the case has been approved by Washington the Consul can accept a new application from the immigrant here."[48] If there had been any doubt before, it was now obvious to the refugees that America had closed its doors.

Second to the United States as the preferred destination was Palestine. Hopes were dimmed, however, because "the British White Paper policy was being applied ruthlessly," according to Zorach Warhaftig.[49] Between October 1940 and June 1941, British authorities did not issue a single

new Palestine permit to Jewish refugees in Japan. Fortunately, most of the refugees who had already been guaranteed certificates in Lithuania were able to collect them in Japan.[50] Now they still faced the arduous trek from Japan to Palestine. Most followed circuitous routes that necessitated coordinating transit visas with transportation, which was often costly. A total of 262 refugees set out for Palestine from Japan.[51]

With more than a thousand refugees in Japan looking for permanent havens by early 1941, Jewcom's staff was overwhelmed and sought assistance from other organiza-

4TH PALESTINE GROUP
FROM KOBE JAPAN
8 VIII 1941

tions, including the Palestine Commission. After opening an office in Kobe, HICEM cooperated with Jewcom in emigration matters.[52] And in the spring of 1941, Vaad ha-Hatzala sent a young American businessman, Frank Newman, to Kobe to arrange the emigration of rabbis and yeshiva students and their families from Japan. Help also came from the embassy of the Polish government-in-exile in Japan, where Ambassador Tadeusz Romer "did his utmost in the matter of obtaining visas to the British Dominions," according to a Jewcom report.[53] Assisted by the Polish Relief Committee, Jewcom, and HICEM, Romer secured some 340 visas to destinations in Canada, Burma, Australia, and New Zealand.[54]

Exploring all options for visas, the refugees' advocates appealed to Dutch diplomats stationed in Japan. In a letter of February 19, 1941, to Dutch Deputy Consul Nicolaas A. J. de Voogd in Kobe, Ponevejsky wrote, "People at the Jewish organizations propose to appeal to the Netherlands authorities to obtain permission to accept a few hundred refugees in their colonies."[55] De Voogd sent the letter to his superior in Tokyo, who duly forwarded it to the Dutch government-in-exile in London, but nothing ever came of the request to allow the refugees to actually enter Curaçao.

Despite the best efforts of the refugee relief and emigration committees, the pace of departures from Japan did not keep up with the pace of arrivals. The delays had serious repercussions for refugees yet to arrive. As Ponevejsky noted, "Thousands of refugees remain in Soviet Russia and will receive Japanese visas only in proportion to the departures of those previously arrived here. Therefore, even if we had the means

Members of the 4th Palestine Group on the eve of their departure for Palestine via Shanghai, August 2, 1941. *USHMM, Gift of Rebeka Ilutovich*

and authority to keep refugees here for months, such a course would prevent other unfortunates from passing through."[56]

Jewcom and the refugees' other advocates in Japan continued to work feverishly to find other places of safety. In April 1941, Rose Shoshana Kahan expressed sentiments typical of those in Kobe unable to get visas: "The time limit for the Japanese transit visa has expired a long time ago; the refugees run about with the question on their lips: What will happen? When?"[57]

TO SHANGHAI

In April 1941, Moses Beckelman cabled the Joint's New York office from Tokyo:

> JAPANESE CONSULATES EUROPE SUSPENDED
> TRANSIT ISSUANCE BELIEVES OVERCOMABLE
> ONLY AFTER SUBSTANTIAL EMIGRATION

PRESENT REFUGEES JAPAN. . . . POLISH CIRCLES BELIEVE SHANGHAI MOVEMENT ADEQUATE REOPEN JAPANESE TRANSIT.[58]

With most options cut off, Jewcom began to turn to a destination of last resort— Shanghai, China. In the 1930s, Shanghai was the only port in the world that did not require an entry visa, and, as a result, it attracted thousands of German and Austrian Jews fleeing Nazi persecution. But following the flood of Jewish refugees from

Nazi Germany after *Kristallnacht* (November 9–10, 1938), Japanese authorities—who won control of the harbor in 1937 during Sino-Japanese fighting—restricted entry, all but closing the port. After August 1939, anyone seeking to enter Shanghai needed to obtain a certificate of permission.

In February 1941, at Jewcom's request, Palestine Commission leader Warhaftig, his colleague Eliezer Szczupakiewicz, and Frank Newman of the Vaad journeyed to

Shanghai. They were to make arrangements not only for the refugees in Japan but also for Polish Jews still stranded in Lithuania. Warhaftig was hopeful that their efforts to obtain entry permit certificates for this latter group would yield results. He wrote to his wife:

> Yesterday we submitted our first list for 100 Shanghai entry permits. Tomorrow we shall hand over the second list, to be followed by a third that we will send from

The Refugee Tragedy
Thousands Hopelessly Jam War Ports Seeking Freedom

Victims of war and oppression on the continents of Europe and Asia have but three possible avenues of escape—and all are closed today.

This was the statement of Moses W. Beckelman, since 1939 a European director of the American joint distribution committee of relief to refugees, upon his arrival here yesterday aboard the S. S. President Coolidge.

He painted a graphic picture of these three bottlenecks through which some 18,000 refugees have fled to the peace and security of the North and South American continents during the last year.

Five thousand refugees wander aimlessly today in Kobe, Japan, awaiting precious papers for entrance to America.

Twice that number are at Lisbon, Portugal, awaiting accommodations aboard the one American passenger line still maintaining service there.

20,000 IN SHANGHEAI

And in Shanghai, "port of last resort," are 20,000 uprooted souls—without hope of escape or means of livelihood, dependent upon international relief organizations such as the one Beckelman represents.

nished by the President Coolidge herself, which stopped at both of those ports en route here and still arrived with but "maybe ten" refu-

MOSES W. BECKELMAN
He talks of bottlenecks

STRANDED

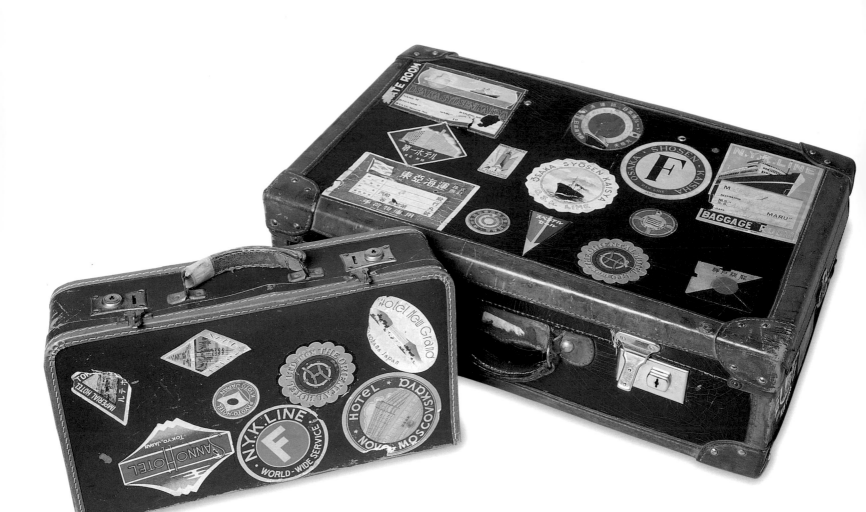

The larger of these two suitcases belonged to Samuel Fishbain, who left Japan for Harbin, Manchuria, to join his brother, a businessman there. The smaller suitcase was carried to Vancouver, British Columbia, in May 1941 by the Fishaut family, who received a visa with the help of the Polish ambassador to Tokyo, Tadeusz Romer. *Sandra, Jeffrey, and Arron Fishbain, family of Samuel Fishbain, Ontario; Dr. Mark Fishaut, New York*

Japan. Should we succeed in bringing out 300 families from Vilna, our month-long separation will have been justified.[59]

Warhaftig later estimated that a total of 400 permits were sent to Kaunas or Moscow.[60] One group of about 50 emigrants did arrive in Shanghai via Vladivostok in May.[61] A month later, the Germans invaded the Soviet Union, and all exits were blocked. No precise statistics exist for the number of refugees who were able to avail themselves of the permits to travel directly from Soviet territory to Shanghai before the invasion.[62]

Meanwhile, emigration from Kobe to Shanghai proceeded slowly. Refugees in Japan for the most part resisted going to Shanghai, because they believed it to be a steamingly hot, corrupt, and crowded city, with few prospects for employment, adequate housing, or escape. In May 1941, Jewcom's Jechel Lewin reported to Ponevejsky, then en route to the United States:

For the moment, as you know it yourself too well, people "sentenced" to go to Shanghai do what they can to defend themselves, and probably they are right, because awful news comes from Shanghai about the treatment and "relief" of refugees over there.[63]

The most resistant to another move were the rabbis and yeshiva students. In June, Lewin, now head of Jewcom, wrote his predecessor, Ponevejsky, about the hundreds of religious scholars still in Japan: "Generally speaking these people are those who do not leave stubbornly waiting for American visas which are available to a small extent only."[64] Two months later, Ponevejsky learned of the continuing intractability: "This group will have to leave for Shanghai, but we are still encountering their stiff resistance and negative attitude."[65]

World events eventually left the refugees still in Japan with no other option but Shanghai. In July 1941, Japanese forces occu-

140

pied French Indochina. The United States responded by imposing an oil embargo and freezing all Japanese assets. The Joint now could no longer transfer funds to Jewcom. As international tensions rose, all passenger routes from Japan to North and South America, Australia, and India were terminated. In mid-August, the Japanese government instructed all foreigners to leave the country. As Leo Hanin recalled, Japanese military authorities came to Jewcom's offices "and told us that the refugees had to leave for Shanghai."[66] Soon after, the Japanese expelled the remaining group of refugees, sending them to Shanghai. Among the last to leave were the entire student body and

faculty of the Mir Yeshiva, who arrived in Shanghai on the eve of the Jewish High Holy Days in late August 1941.[67]

To the last days of their stay in Kobe, Shanghai was much dreaded. In August 1941, Rose Shoshana Kahan wrote: "We have to go to Shanghai. Terrible letters come from there. One runs again to see if our names are on the list to leave. Before, when one saw his name on the list, one was happy. Today, when one sees his name on the piece of paper to be sent to Shanghai, one cries."[67] In October, the Kahans could not avoid the inevitable: "On October 20th we travel to Shanghai. We are about the last."[69]

THE OSAKA MAINICHI & THE TO[KYO NICHI NICHI]

Jewish Refugees Leave Kobe For Shanghai

KOBE, Aug. 20.—Approximately 300 local Jewish refugees, consisting mostly of students of the Jewish religion, sailed for Shanghai at noon today to proceed to their new homes. With their departure, the Jewish refugee population here has been reduced to around 550.

foreigners that had been here on vacation that also left.

Among the residents sailing were J. L. Saravia, Bolivian consul-general at Yokohama, and his wife; Mr. Janning, relative of the famed actor Emil Janning, and his family; and A. R. Lanney, buyer, en route to Shanghai.

Osaka Mainichi & Tokyo Nichi Nichi, August 21, 1941

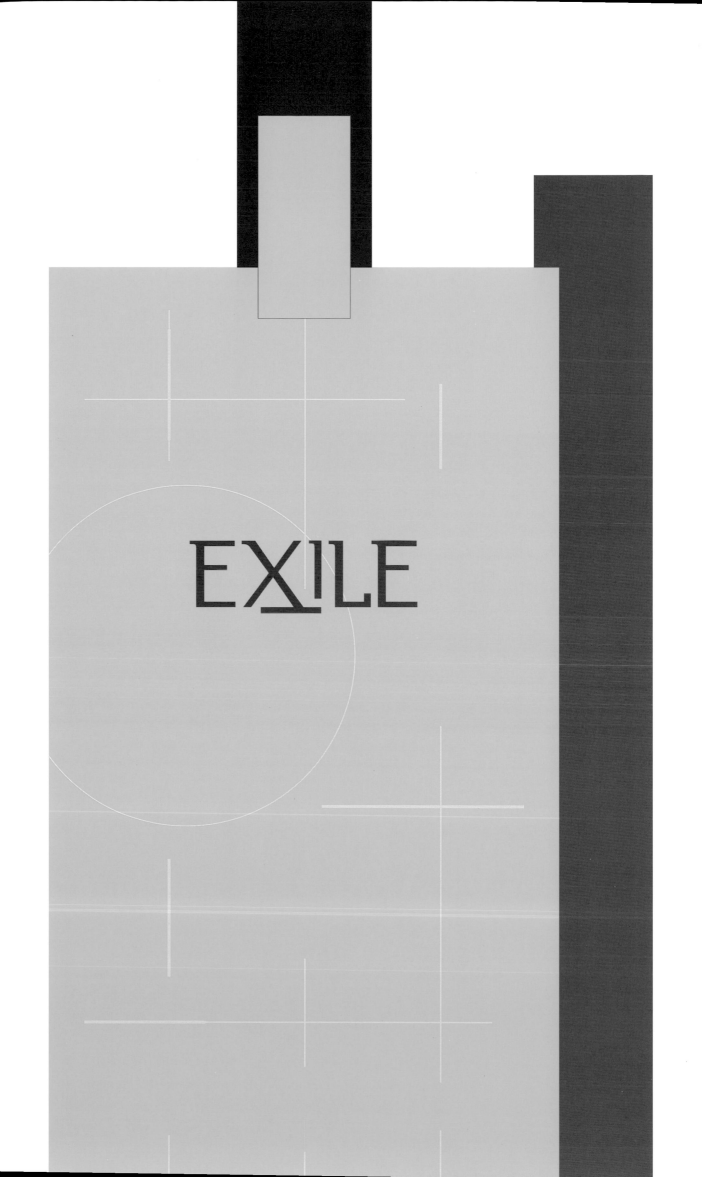

7 EXILE

FINAL REFUGE IN SHANGHAI

After two days at sea, the refugees forced to leave Japan caught their first glimpse of Shanghai as their steamers approached the shallow, muddy Whangpoo River that leads to the city's harbor. "Everyone was in shock at what we saw," Hanni Sondheimer Vogelweid recalled. "We'd never dreamt it would look like it did. We never had any idea what China was about, how poor it was."[1] Oil storage tanks and warehouses dotted the shore. Beyond lay rubble and buildings destroyed during the Sino-Japanese hostilities of 1937. Farther along the shore, the dismal industrial wasteland gave way to skyscrapers lining the Bund, Shanghai's famous harborside roadway. Shanghai was a city of striking contrasts.

In the years preceding World War II, Shanghai was a divided city. In 1842, when the then-minor port was opened to western trade, Great Britain, the United States, France, Italy, and Portugal established extraterritorial rights in the city's so-called foreign concessions—the International Settlement, administered by a municipal council of Western powers, and the French Concession, headed by the French consul general. By the 1930s, many of Shanghai's business establishments and foreign consulates were located in the modern office buildings of the International Settlement. "Frenchtown," with its wide, tree-lined boulevards, elegant residences, and exclusive shops, was home to most of Shanghai's wealthier residents.

Before the arrival of Jews fleeing Nazi persecution and the war in Europe, the International Settlement and French Concession were home to two main Jewish groups. The older and smaller group consisted of about 700 Sephardic Jews whose fathers and grandfathers had arrived from

ABOVE: Jewish refugees and Chinese vendors on Chusan Road, Hongkew, 1940s. *USHMM, courtesy of Horst Eisfelder*

RIGHT: Destitute Chinese man lies in front of Café Max, which was operated by Jewish refugees in Hongkew, 1940s. *USHMM, courtesy of Horst Eisfelder*

Iraq as traders in the mid-1800s and quickly ascended the social and economic ladder.[2] Most of the Sephardic Jews were educated in British schools, and many held British citizenship. "Sir Victor," patriarch of the fabulously wealthy Sassoon clan, was the Sephardic community's unofficial leader and would become one of the refugees' most generous benefactors. The second and larger community comprised a few thousand Ashkenazi Jews who had fled to China as refugees from Russia during the Revolution of 1917. Most of them earned modest livings as small business owners. The Russian Jews would feel a natural affinity with the Polish Jews, who brought the cultural and religious trappings of eastern European Jewry from which they had been isolated for so many years.

In the aftermath of the 1937 Sino-Japanese fighting, large sections of Shanghai fell under Japanese control, including the part of the International Settlement referred to as Hongkew. Japanese marines—the Naval Landing Party—patrolled these sections and the harbor. Violent battles during the conflict had reduced much of industrial Hongkew to rubble-strewn lots and gutted buildings. Chinese laborers and impoverished Russian and Japanese residents lived in the buildings that remained intact.

"All of 'Hongkew' presents itself as a terrible portrait," wrote Rose Shoshana Kahan after she scouted the area for cheap lodging in October 1941. "Dilapidated houses, ruins from bombs, skeletons of former factories, and bombed out shops."[3] New arrivals heard a cacophony of unfamiliar languages and smelled unfamiliar cooking aromas and the stench of rotting garbage and human waste. In Hongkew, "death was an everyday event," recalled Norbert Swislocki. Each morning the streets were littered with dead bodies—the forgotten Chinese underclass, who succumbed to the damp cold of winter, the unrelenting heat and humidity of summer, and hunger and disease all year long.[4]

GERMAN AND AUSTRIAN JEWISH REFUGEES

When the Jews from Poland arrived in 1941, they joined a much larger refugee community. An estimated 17,000 German and Austrian Jews had first trickled into Shanghai after the beginning of Nazi persecution of Jews in 1933, and then, following the 1938 violence of *Kristallnacht*, streamed in like a flood. Unlike most of the Polish Jews, these early refugees had usually immigrated to Shanghai as families. Stripped of most of their assets before fleeing the Reich, these thousands of refugees swarmed into Hongkew because they could not afford to live anywhere else in the foreign concessions.

During the 1930s, Nazi policy encouraged Jewish emigration from Germany, and a ship's passage enabled a person to gain release, even from a concentration camp. At first, Shanghai seemed an unlikely refuge, but as it became clear that most countries in

Dr. Heinrich Mannes, a refugee dentist in Shanghai. *USHMM, Gift of John and Harriet Isaack*

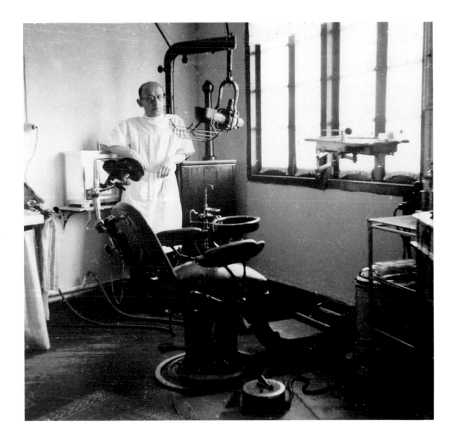

EXILE

Most refugee doctors and dentists in Shanghai had difficulty making a living. To economize, they shared office space, as the hours posted on these signs indicate. *Courtesy of the Leo Baeck Institute, New York*

Erwin Eisfelder at the Café Louis, which was operated by his family. It was a popular gathering place for refugees in Shanghai during the war years. *USHMM, courtesy of Horst Eisfelder*

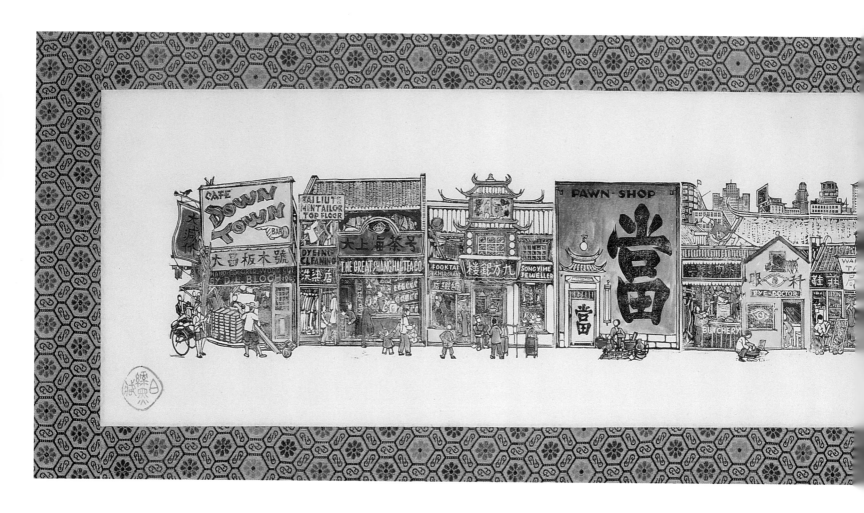

ABOVE: David Bloch, untitled woodblock print with watercolor, c.1945. Bloch, a German Jewish refugee, depicted typical shops in "Little Vienna," as Chusan Road in Hongkew became known. *David L. Bloch, New York*

RIGHT: Artist David Bloch. In November 1938 he was interned for several weeks in the Dachau concentration camp near Munich. With the help of his brother in the United States, he escaped from Germany to Shanghai in May 1940. *David L. Bloch, New York*

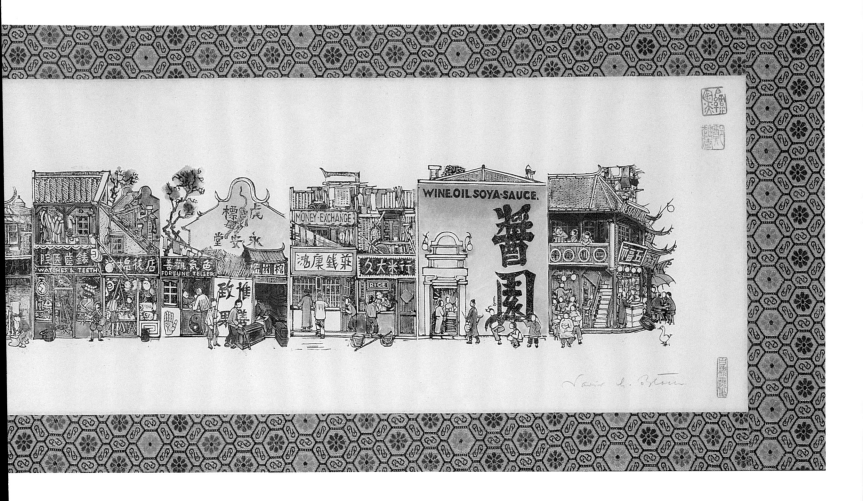

the world were limiting or denying entry to Jews, it became the only available choice. Until August 1939, no visas were required for entering Shanghai. Ernest Heppner, who fled Breslau with his mother in 1939, recalled that "[the] main thing was to get out of Germany, and really at this point, people did not care where we went, anywhere just to get away from Germany."[5]

Arrival in Shanghai was a shock, especially for those who had just stepped off a European liner on which they had been served breakfast by uniformed stewards and now found themselves lining up for lunch in a soup kitchen. "Nothing demonstrated more clearly the drastic change that had taken place in our lives than the sight of us dressed in our good, heavy European clothing, the women still adorned with fashionable hats and gloves, waiting in line with tin pots in hand for our next meal," remembered Heppner.[6] Once the refugees settled in, finding

work was a challenge, and many refugees had to rely on at least some charitable relief.

Still, the majority of German and Austrian Jews managed. Despite the blows to Shanghai's economy dealt by the Sino-Japanese conflict, some of them adapted remarkably well, taking advantage of the opportunities that the city had always offered to hard-working, enterprising individuals. The Eisfelder family, whose son Horst was 13 when they arrived at the end of 1938, opened and operated Café Louis, a popular gathering place for refugees throughout the war years.[7] Others established small factories or cottage industries, set themselves up as doctors or teachers, found jobs with local businesses, or worked as architects or builders to transform sections of bombed-out Hongkew. By 1940, an area around Chusan Road was known as "Little Vienna," owing to its European-style cafés, delicatessens, nightclubs, shops, and bakeries.

ABOVE: Goblets used in Shanghai by the Caspary family for blessings (Kiddush) over wine on the Sabbath and Jewish holidays. The Casparys were Orthodox Jews who operated a kosher restaurant frequented by yeshiva students from Poland. *The Zalcgendler Family, New York*

LEFT: Boy Scout scarf and handmade badges worn by German Jewish refugee children. British expatriates had transplanted the Boy Scout organization to Shanghai many years before the refugees' arrival. *USHMM, Gift of Eric Bergtraun; Günter (Gary) Matzdorff, California*

REFUGEE RELIEF EFFORTS

When Shanghai's refugee population suddenly jumped from about 1,500 at the end of 1938 to nearly 17,000 one year later, the local Jews were overwhelmed and hard-pressed to find the resources to help needy families. The Committee for Assistance of European Jewish Refugees in Shanghai, formed in 1938 by prominent local Jews, turned to the Joint Distribution Committee in New York for additional funds. The JDC appropriation rose from $5,000 in 1938 to $100,600 in 1939. Even this barely kept up with the mounting demands. By late 1939, more than half of the refugee population required financial help for food or housing.[8]

The Committee for Assistance established five group shelters for a minority of totally impoverished German and Austrian Jews. Although the shelters were called *Heime* ("homes" in German), they were not homelike. The Ward Road *Heim* that opened in January 1939 was hastily converted from a former barracks and outfitted with hard, narrow bunk beds under which the residents stored their few belongings. By the end of 1939, about 2,500 people lived in the *Heime*, sleeping anywhere from six to 150 to a room.[9] The Joint's representative, Laura Margolis, reported, "The so-called '*Heimes*' were a terrific shock. In some of them the refugees are so crowded; the atmosphere so depressing; and the people look so completely hopeless and lost that one visit is enough to know that ultimately this condition must be alleviated."[10] An additional 4,500 individuals ate in soup kitchens set up in the *Heime* but lived elsewhere in rented rooms. Many of them received relief help to pay for part or all of their housing costs.[11]

Margolis had been detailed to Shanghai in 1941 to help American consular staff process visas to the United States. One month after arriving, however, she had to cope with the State Department's new visa regulations denying entry to refugees with relatives in the occupied territories. Since the crippling restrictions disqualified most of the refugees Margolis had been screening, she redirected her efforts to organizing relief activities.[12] This brought her into contact with the Polish Jews who were arriving from Japan. From the start, they steadfastly refused to live in the degrading *Heime*. The Polish Jews felt that cultural, social, and religious differences between the two refugee groups made joint housing impractical. They also strongly resisted being categorized with the German and Austrian Jews, who held passports issued by the Reich and were therefore regarded as enemy aliens by the British and their allies in the International Settlement. The Polish Jewish refugees wanted to be treated as allies by the Polish and British consuls in the hope of getting assistance to leave Shanghai.[13]

Refugees share cramped quarters in a *Heim* (home) in Shanghai, c.1946. *United Nations Archives and Record Center, New York*

RIGHT: **People line up for food at the soup kitchen of the Ward Road refugee home in Shanghai, which was funded by the American Jewish Joint Distribution Committee.** *Ullstein Bilder-dienst, Berlin*

OPPOSITE: **Frau Schoenberg with her belongings, including a sewing machine shipped from Germany. Despite her shabby, cramped quarters in Shanghai, she tried to create a semblance of her former domestic life.** *USHMM, Gift of John and Harriet Isaack*

Laura Margolis
(1903–1997)

Born in Turkey to parents of German-Jewish extraction, Laura Margolis spoke French, German, Greek, and Turkish by the age of five. In 1908, she and her family went to Dayton, Ohio, where she learned English and Spanish. Her facility with languages served her well when she later became active in international relief work.

Trained as a social worker at Case Western Reserve University, she embarked on a career in Jewish social services, first in Cleveland and then in New York. In 1937, she went to Havana to assist Jewish refugees from Germany attempting to enter Cuba.

The American Jewish Joint Distribution Committee sent Margolis to China in 1941. She spent more than two years in Shanghai, including six months in a Japanese internment camp as an enemy national. Released in August 1943 as part of a prisoner exchange, she returned to New York.

The Joint sought to persuade Margolis, still recovering from her captivity, to undertake less demanding work in Santo Domingo. Eschewing inaction, she headed to England and Sweden to help direct the Joint's refugee programs and later became the first female director of the Joint in France. She and her husband, a French journalist, settled in Israel in 1953.

PHOTO: *American Jewish Joint Distribution Committee Archives, Jerusalem, courtesy of Beth Hatefutsoth Photo Archive, Israel*

The 300 students and rabbis of the Mir Yeshiva presented a special case. They had maintained their rigorous study schedule during the odyssey that had taken them from Poland to Japan. Now, in Shanghai, a suitable place where they could study and pray had to be found. As it happened, the elegant Beth Aharon Synagogue, a spacious, two-story building constructed under the patronage of Silas A. Hardoon, a wealthy Sephardic Jew, stood empty and unused. A yeshiva student recalled the sense that fate had led them to Beth Aharon:

> When the yeshiva members saw all this magnificence . . . as though awaiting their arrival, and when they discovered that the three hundred-odd seats in the sanctu-

ary matched the exact number of students, they were convinced that it was indeed another miracle of Divine Providence. The edifice had been built just for them.[14]

For the first few weeks, the Mir students studied in the synagogue during the day, placing mattresses on the floor to sleep at night. Over time, with the help of the Joint, Vaad ha-Hatzala, and a local committee guided by the Shanghai Jews' spiritual leader, Rabbi Meier Ashkenazi, the Mir students eventually found living quarters. Zlota Ginsburg, the wife of a Mir student, later recalled the cramped accommodations: "My parents and sister lived in the same room with my husband and me and the children. We divided the room with a

ישיבת־מיר כעת בשנגהי
בבהמ״ד בית־אחרן, מוזעאום רד. 50 שנת תש״ב

OPPOSITE: Decorative block
from the facade of the Beth
Aharon Synagogue in Shanghai. During the demolition of
the building in 1985, it was
preserved to memorialize the
wartime haven that Shanghai
provided for yeshiva students
and other Jewish refugees.
*Shanghai Museum, Shanghai;
photograph by Peter Harholdt*

ABOVE: Students and rabbis of
the Mir Yeshiva, led by Rabbi
Chakiel Lewensztejn (front
row, far left) and Rabbi Lejba
Szmuelowicz (front row,
second from right), gather in
the study hall at the Beth
Aharon Synagogue, Shanghai,
1941. *Rabbi Jacob Ederman,
New York*

LEFT: Beth Aharon
Synagogue on Museum Road,
Shanghai. *Beth Hatefutsoth
Photo Archive, Israel, courtesy
of Rose Horowitz, Los Angeles*

curtain, and there was a little stove with which to heat and cook."[15]

Many refugees shared quarters in tiny row houses that lined the dark, narrow alleys running off Chusan Road and other main streets of Hongkew. The houses equipped with indoor plumbing had only one toilet, shared by all the residents; in those without, residents used buckets, emptied each morning by Chinese laborers.[16] The typical refugee diet was plain and monotonous, largely consisting of inexpensive but filling foods—rice, noodles, or potatoes, occasionally flavored with a bit of chicken, fish, or sugar.

PEARL HARBOR

On December 8, 1941, residents of Shanghai were abruptly awakened at 4 A.M. by naval gunfire. Japanese forces had attacked the United States naval base at Pearl Harbor in Hawaii. (On the other side of the international date line, it was still December 7.) Simultaneous attacks were launched all over the South Pacific, and in Shanghai, Japanese warships sank the British gunboat HMS *Petrel*. Japanese military forces proceeded to occupy the entire city without incident. That day Rose Shoshana Kahan noted in her diary:

> What will happen now? We are again in the fire of war. Dear God, have we not suffered enough? This morning the Pacific War broke out. Japan and America. There is no longer any piece of earth in this entire world where it is peaceful. All our friends run around in a state of confusion.... Now we are stuck here.... Tossed into an Asian land.... Who knows what may still happen to us.[17]

The Japanese occupation shocked and frightened the refugees. Like almost everyone else in Shanghai, Motl Goldberg awoke to the sounds of predawn explosions. He rushed to the window and in the dim morning light was able to make out bayonet-

OPPOSITE: Polish yeshiva students in Shanghai. *USHMM, courtesy of Horst Eisfelder*

ABOVE: Many Jewish refugees lived in small apartments off alleys like this one near Chusan Road, Hongkew. *USHMM, courtesy of Horst Eisfelder*

LEFT: Ration stamps issued to the Jewish refugees in Shanghai during the war, listing the shops where purchases could be made. *Dr. Norbert I. Swislocki, New York*

wielding Japanese soldiers standing on the corner. Terror-stricken, he remained inside his apartment for three days, under strict orders given by Japanese soldiers.[18] The situation created great uncertainty among the Polish refugees. Yonia Fain recalled his doubts and fears after Pearl Harbor: "We didn't know what was going to happen. We didn't know how we were going to survive. We didn't know how the Japanese would treat us. Everything was very, very confusing."[19]

By the time of the Japanese attack, only a handful of the nearly 1,000 Polish Jews had managed to leave the city and move on to other destinations. Leon Pommers, a concert pianist, was one of the fortunate few. While in Kobe, he had obtained a Canadian visa with the help of Polish Ambassador

Romer and spent only six weeks in Shanghai. Just before leaving, he performed George Gershwin's "Rhapsody in Blue" at the Carlton Theatre, and in October 1941 sailed to Canada via Australia.[20] But the vast majority of refugees were not so lucky. Japan's entry into the war now dashed their hopes of escape, leaving them stranded in Shanghai indefinitely.

In January 1942, the Japanese leadership reformulated Japan's four-year-old policy toward Jews. It had been assumed at the 1938 Five Ministers Conference that Jewish international power and influence could be turned to favor Japan's interests. Now the "emergency situation" created by the "Greater East Asia War" superseded such considerations. Jews could no longer broker relations between Japan, Great Britain,

Japanese naval forces march on Nanjing Road in the International Settlement, Shanghai, December 8, 1941. *Courtesy of the Leo Baeck Institute, New York*

ABOVE: Shanghai Municipal Council entry certificates that Leon Pomeraniec obtained in 1941 for his mother and sister after he arrived in Shanghai. They were unable to leave Poland and later perished in the Holocaust. *Leon Pommers, New York*

LEFT: The Japanese report "Jewish Measures in View of the Situation in 1942" modified the policy established at the Five Ministers Conference in 1938. After the outbreak of the Pacific war, Jews were no longer considered useful to Japan. However, total "rejection of the Jewish people" was viewed as contrary to national policy and likely to stimulate anti-Japanese propaganda by the Allied nations. *Japanese Foreign Ministry Diplomatic Record Office, Tokyo*

and the United States, nor could they direct foreign capital to Japan.[21]

Given the exigencies of war, the new policy ordered that Jews in Japanese-occupied territories be "handled according to citizenship." In a cable dated January 15, 1942, Japan's consuls in China were given three new instructions. First, German Jews in China were to be treated as "stateless persons," because Germany had abolished the citizenship of Jews living overseas as of January 1, 1942. Second, Jewish citizens of neutral countries who could be useful to the Japanese should be treated "favorably." Third, all other Jews should be monitored "strictly" for any activities conducted "on behalf of the enemy." But despite the fact that its Axis allies, Germany and Italy, enforced an "anti-Jewish policy," Japan would not "drive out the Jews completely." Such a course of action was viewed as contrary to the Japanese ideal of world unification ("the eight corners of the earth under one roof"). It also might fuel anti-

Japanese propaganda by Great Britain and the United States.[22]

The modified Japanese policy toward Jews initially affected only those who were enemy nationals, but their treatment had ramifications for Jewish refugees viewed as stateless. Immediately following the occupation of Shanghai, British and Dutch citizens had to register with Japanese authorities and display posters in their places of business identifying themselves as enemy nationals. Occupation authorities installed Japanese managers in their businesses, confiscated their property, and froze their bank accounts. Consequently, the Sassoons, the Abrahams, and other wealthy Sephardic families who held British passports could no longer support the Jewish refugee relief effort. In the fall of 1942, enemy nationals were required to wear identifying red armbands.[23]

The war also affected the status of relief funds. With the outbreak of war with Japan,

the Joint ceased transmitting money to Shanghai, in accordance with the Anglo-American Trading with the Enemy Act. As a result, local relief committees drastically reduced their assistance allotments. Those refugees who had relied on American relatives were now cut off as well. Hanni Sondheimer Vogelweid said that when she and her family arrived in Shanghai, "we had money, we could buy things, we could eat things that we liked. But the moment the [Pacific] war started, then all contact was gone with America. Things got rough."[24]

The refugees' situation grew precarious. Faced with a crisis, Laura Margolis and her colleague Manuel Siegel approached a Japanese official, Captain Koreshige Inuzuka, who headed the Bureau for Jewish Affairs in Shanghai. They asked him for three things: permission to secure loans that would be backed by the Joint's guarantee, the unfreezing of relief funds, and the release of 5,000 bags of wheat sent to the refugees by the American Red Cross, which the Japanese had confiscated. Margolis argued, "You, as an occupying power, cannot afford to have hungry people riot. You're responsible for them. On the other hand, I can help you so they won't riot, if you'll give me an okay to raise the money." To Margolis's surprise, Inuzuka agreed to all the requests. By April 1942, with the Joint's guarantee, she had raised $180,000; she obtained additional loans on the basis of nothing more than promises of reimbursement.[25] Margolis and Siegel's relief work ended in early 1943, when they were interned as enemy nationals along with 7,500 British, American, and other civilians. Margolis was among about 1,000 other British and American men, women, and children detained in the Chapei camp, located in a Shanghai university.[26]

The Pacific war isolated the Jewish refugee community even further from events in Europe. Japanese authorities shut down or censored local Shanghai newspapers and cut off overseas mail service. Sigmund Tobias, who had come to Shanghai as a child, remembered the long summer evenings when the adults sat outside trying to keep cool, while they circulated "the latest local rumors, discussed the events of the day, or examined over and over again the news from Europe. The most frightening topic was what might be happening to the relatives we had left behind."[27] In the absence of uncensored news, the refugees' knowledge of the war and Nazi occupation came in half-truths, rumors, and reports in the Soviet press.[28] In late 1942, the Soviet newspapers contained stories about deportations from the Warsaw ghetto.[29] This information and fragments of reports and intelligence that trickled into Shanghai raised the refugees' fears about their loved ones back home. At the beginning of 1943, Rose Shoshana Kahan recorded in her diary, "Frightening rumors are circulating regarding Poland. We don't know exactly what or when."[30]

THE "DESIGNATED AREA"

Against the backdrop of the refugees' growing emotional and physical vulnerability, Japanese authorities dropped "a bombshell" on the community.[31] On February 18, 1943, a military proclamation ordered entire categories of refugees to relocate and stay within a designated area in Hongkew. The proclamation read: "Due to military necessity, places of residence and business of the stateless refugees in the Shanghai area shall hereafter be restricted to the undermentioned area in the International Settlement." The restricted zone was a small area in one of the poorer parts of Hongkew. Refugees were to relocate by May 18.[32]

The proclamation left undefined the term "stateless refugees," but the meaning was clarified in the Shanghai newspapers. All refugees "who arrived in Shanghai since 1937 from Germany (including former Austria,

OPPOSITE, TOP: Proclamation issued on February 18, 1943, by the Imperial Japanese Army and Navy authorities establishing, for reasons of "military necessity," a "designated area" for "stateless refugees" in the Hongkew area of the International Settlement. *USHMM, courtesy of Eric Goldstaub*

OPPOSITE, BOTTOM: License to Removal issued by Japanese authorities in 1943 to Elias Kupinsky for the transfer of his business to the restricted district of Hongkew in Shanghai. *Hirsh Kupinsky, Ontario*

Czecho-Slovakia), Hungary, former Poland, Latvia, Lithuania and Estonia, etc. and who have no nationality at present" were deemed "stateless" and assigned to the "designated area." Most of the Russian Jews were, in fact, "stateless," as was the sizable White Russian population, but both of these groups were exempted to avoid "international complications"—friction with the Soviet Union.[33] Japan had signed a neutrality pact with the USSR in 1941 and was reluctant to jeopardize the military security provided by the agreement.

Nazi officials in Shanghai, which had a large German expatriate community, constantly made efforts to stir up anti-Jewish propaganda in Japanese circles.[34] In Berlin, at a meeting with Tokyo's Ambassador Hiroshi Oshima on May 7, 1942, Alfred Rosenberg, the Reich Minister for the Occupied Eastern Territories, discussed the need to isolate the Jews in Shanghai.[35] But there is no documentation linking these efforts in Shanghai or Berlin to the establishment of the restricted area. In fact, after the 1943 proclamation was announced, the German consul general in Shanghai, Martin Fischer, expressed his surprise in reports to the German Foreign Office in Berlin and indicated that he had not received advance notice of the move.[36]

When Japanese authorities interned enemy nationals, they used the foreigners' own organizations to mobilize the internment. Thus they depended on the Russian Jewish community to set up the restricted area and implement the move. A newly formed Shanghai Ashkenazi Collaborating Relief Association went about this task reluctantly.[37] Approximately 7,500 stateless Jews, including residents in the *Heime,* already lived in the "designated area," together with about 100,000 Chinese. But another 7,500 Jews affected by the proclamation had to find housing and relocate their places of business. The three-month deadline forced refugees to accept less than fair market

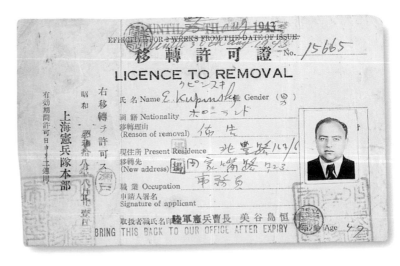

Shanghai, April 23, 1943.

40.3

Sirs,

On behalf of Polish Citizens, holders of valid passports, temporarily residing in Shanghai and affected by the Proclamation of the Imperial Japanese Military Authorities issued on the 18th of February 1943, we have the honour to state that we are under protection of the Polish Residents' Association in China, 41 Route Cohen, as certified by the letter enclosed herewith, and wherein it is also testified that the named Association takes full responsibility for all persons included in the list hereto attached.

In connection with that guarantee we have the honour to request you to kindly exempt us from the effects of the Proclamation by graciously granting permission to retain our present domiciles.

Permit us to express by that opportunity the deepest gratitude which we owe to the Imperial Japanese Consul General in Kaunas, who by granting visas made it possible for us to leave the territory then under control of U.S.S.R., and also to all other Imperial Japanese Authorities for their hospitality during our stay in Kobe for several months and for providing us with permits to Shanghai where we are transient guests until we shall regain the possibility to leave.

It is only due to the outbreak of hostilities in the Far East that not all of us have succeeded in leaving Shanghai and proceeding to their various destinations, as originally intended. Those, however, who were impeded to do so still are awaiting the first repatriation possibility to leave.

Trusting you will give this matter your kind attention and our petition will be favourably considered,

we are, Sirs,

Respectfully Yours,

Letter to Japanese authorities, April 23, 1943, from a group of Polish Jews appealing for exemption from the proclamation issued two months earlier that ordered stateless refugees into a "designated area." The appeal failed. *YIVO Institute for Jewish Research, New York*

prices on their investments. They were further disadvantaged because the lesser-quality lodging available inside the "designated area" usually sold at inflated prices. The result was not only the loss of financial independence but also new living quarters that were often smaller than where they had been residing.[38]

In one instance, the forced relocation met some resistance. In April 1943, a group of

Polish Jews appealed to Japanese authorities for special exemption, making reference to earlier Japanese kindnesses:

> Permit us to express . . . the deepest gratitude which we owe to the Imperial Japanese Consul General in Kaunas, who by granting visas made it possible for us to leave the territory then under control of U.S.S.R. and also to all other Imperial Japanese authorities for their hospitality during our stay in Kobe for several months and for providing us with permits to Shanghai where we are transient guests until we shall regain the possibility to leave.[39]

The petition suggested that since the refugees were under the protection of the Polish Residents' Association in China, they should be classified as Polish citizens. Knowing full well that citizenship would result in internment, the group hoped that enemy national status would bring the protection of the Red Cross and the prospect of repatriation. But the letter of appeal fell on deaf ears, and Japanese authorities ordered the group into the restricted area.

A handful of defiant Polish refugees continued to hold out successfully until March 1944, when they were incarcerated by Japanese authorities. While in jail, 12 contracted typhus, and six died from the disease soon after being released. All of the men had received visas from Sugihara in 1940.[40]

The Japanese authorities also had to contend with a number of Mir Yeshiva students who resisted the forced relocation, protesting the move by smashing furniture in the relief association's offices. The Japanese arrested and imprisoned the students. Their release was secured only through the intervention of Rabbi Ashkenazi.[41] Now forced to live within the restricted zone, the students were nonetheless granted permission to study by day at the Beth Aharon Synagogue, located outside the "designated area."

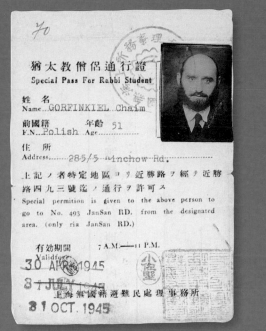

STATELESS REFUGEES ARE PROHIBITED TO PASS HERE WITHOUT PERMISSION

The refugees very soon called the restricted area a "ghetto." But the "designated area" was not walled or fenced off, and the Japanese never subjected the Jews to forced labor and the other radical measures adopted in Nazi ghettos in Europe. The Shanghai ghetto residents also had more freedom of movement than the Japanese allowed enemy nationals forced into internment camps elsewhere. Exit from the area was permitted and controlled by a pass system. Japanese sentries were posted at the ghetto's exit points, as were members of the Jewish civilian guard. Known as the *Pao Chia*, such citywide units had been organized as an auxiliary police force by the Japanese in 1942. Male refugees found most degrading the requirement to serve several hours weekly in rotating shifts as

ABOVE: Feared by the refugees for his cruel and erratic behavior, Japanese administrator Kanoh Ghoya of the Bureau of Stateless Refugees Affairs was in charge of distributing passes to those who wanted to leave the restricted area. *Ernest G. Heppner, Indiana*

RIGHT: Pass issued by Japanese authorities allowing the bearer to leave the "designated area" during the day. *USHMM, Gift of Leo Arnfeld*

Pao Chia guards, but most complied, fearing reprisals if they refused.[42]

Japanese civil administrators in the Bureau of Stateless Refugees Affairs enforced the restrictions. Kanoh Ghoya and his colleague, Okura, controlled the exit passes. "In theory a pass was available on demand," observed one refugee. "In practice, however, a Jew who asked for one was often subject to violent verbal or physical abuse from the man in charge of issuance. For those who had outside jobs and depended frequently on these passes, this treatment often became an unbearable strain."[43] Ghoya, who called himself the "King of the Jews," was known to be a tyrant. Shorter than most of the refugees, he sometimes climbed onto his desk to give himself stature and slapped the refugees, taunting and terrifying them. The official's outbursts appeared irrational and erratic, as the bewildered refugees would also see him giving small gifts to children or distributing passes freely. Okura's treatment of refugees was equally unpredictable and cruel.[44]

REFUGEE LIFE IN SHANGHAI

Polish Jewish writers had a Yiddish expression to describe Shanghai: *shond khay,* "a shame of a life."[45] Despite such sentiments, however, life went on in this foreign and isolated setting, both before and after the establishment of the restricted area. The reading of Yiddish poems, publication of Yiddish and Polish newspapers, and creation of artwork and plays, though intermittent due to shortages and Japanese censorship, helped sustain the remnant of refugees transplanted from Poland. In addition, occasional income from these activities supplemented the relief funds that most of the refugees needed to survive. Refugee writer Josef Fiszman, for example, sold articles to Jewish newspapers in Shanghai and Harbin but still needed help from the Joint Distribution Committee.[46] Abraham Swislocki, a journalist in Warsaw before

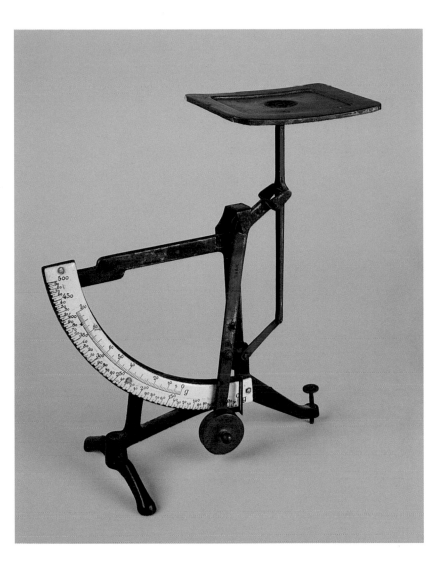

ABOVE: Scale used by refugees Masza Swislocki and George Lieberfreund to weigh jars of artificial honey, which they manufactured and sold in the restricted area. *Dr. Norbert I. Swislocki, New York*

LEFT: Label for the ersatz honey. *Dr. Norbert I. Swislocki, New York*

Artist Yonia Fain with the child Viktor Kirszencwejg (back row, center), who was born near the end of the war. Fain's friends were all from Warsaw, the remnant of the Bundists who escaped from Lithuania. They helped sustain one another during the long years of isolation in Shanghai. *David Kirszencwejg, New York*

the war, wrote articles for Jewish newspapers in Shanghai and briefly published a Polish-language weekly. His wife, Masza, who had been a food-processing chemist in Poland, collaborated with George Lieberfreund, an agricultural engineer by training, to produce and sell ersatz honey concocted from sugar, vanilla, and caramel color.[47] Refugee artist Yonia Fain sold portraits and other paintings and drawings in Shanghai. He staged a solo exhibition of his portraits and participated in a group show during the war years. Fain described these exhibitions, as well as the Yiddish poetry he wrote, as "resistance against despair and nothingness."[48]

Actress Rose Shoshana Kahan remained drawn to the stage even after the Japanese

censors insisted on inspecting each script, and the actors could rehearse only after long days of working or looking for employment. The indefatigable Kahan described her efforts:

> I already knew where the talented amateurs lived. I had to go to their residences to teach them the parts in Yiddish, handle by myself the necessary requirements, direct, play, but I derived great pleasure from the sold out houses, both, because of the material end and because of the artistic side.[49]

Inspired by her audience's enthusiastic response to the productions, Kahan and her fellow actors presented regular performances, including Sholem Aleichem's *Tevye the Milkman,* which she and her

FIRST IN SHANGHAI
Exhibition of Jewish Artists

Inaugurated at the "Jewish Book" Evening on Wednesday, May 5th, 1943 and opened on Thursday, May 6th from 3-8 p.m., on Friday, May 7th from 2-6 p. m. and on Saturday, May 8th from 2-8 p. m.

Programme

I   DAVID LUDWIG BLOCH
   1 (1) The Bund, 2 (2) Geranium, 3 (3) Flowers, 4 (4) Danube Landscape, 5 (5) Bavarian Suburb, 6 (6) Shanghai Suburb, 7 (7) Misrach.

II   MICHAIL BRENNER
   1 (8) Landscape (Hanchow), 2 (9) Autumn Flowers, 3 (10) Portrait (Mme G), 4 (11) Portrait of a Young Man, 5 (12) Sketch of a Chinese, 6 (13) Flowers.

III   JOSEPH FAIN
   1 (14) Grandfather & Child, 2 (15) Jews Playing Chess, 3 (16) Homeless, 4 (17) Flowers, 5 (18) Rabbi & Pupils, 6 (19) Uriel Acosta, 7 (20) Chinese Head, 8 (21) Head of a Beggar.

IV   PAUL FISHER
   1 (22) Chinese Landscape, 2 (23) Java Dancer, 3 (24) Flowers, 4 (25) Old Jew, 5 (26) Arabian Bay, 6 (27) River, 7 (28) Trees, 8 (29) Ex Libris.

V   FRED FREDEN GOLDBERG
   1 (30) Praying Jews, 2 (31) Haluz, 3 (32) Self-Portrait, 4 (33) Flowers.

VI   ERNST HANDEL
   1 (34) Meditation, 2 (35), Still Life (Apples), 3 (26) Glass with Flowers, 4 (37) Vase, 5 (38) Emigrants' home, 6 (39) Portrait.

VII   MAX HEYMAN
   1 (40) Flowers, 2 (41) Landscape 3 (42) Portrait, 4 (43) Friday.

VIII   HANS JACOBI
   1 (44) Mountain Matterhoirn (Switzerland) 2 (45) Chinese Masks, 3 (46) Kwan-yuan, 4 (47) Netherlands Peasant Wedding (copy), 5 (48) Portrait (Lange)– pencil sketch, 6 (49) Portrait (Ling), 7 (50) Portrait (La), 8 (51) Old Jew (pencil sketch).

IX   E. MOSSOWICH
   1 (52) Rabbi of Amshinoff, 2 (53) The Writer late Mr. Liu Sun, 3 (54) Mr. Veng Lay Ding, 4 (55) Return from the Market, 5 (56) Four Chinese Stage Make-ups, 6 (57) Eight Pieces Original Carton for Needle Point Work, 7 (58) Specimen, Gross Point with Original Carton, 8 (58a) Specimen, Petit Point with Original Carton, 9 (58b) Furniture decoration.

X   Z. OKUN-GENKIN
   1 (59) Autumn (copy), 3 (61) Summer (copy), 4 (62) Alley (copy), 5 (63) Landscape (copy).

XI   HELENE ROOTSTEIN
   1 (64) Passover (Still Life), 2 (65) Sketch (Portrait), 3 (66) Still Life.

XII   RACHEL
   1 (67) Portrait (Miss B), 2 (68) Portrait of Father, 3 (69) Portrait of Shvilli, 4 (70) Head of a Girl. 5 (71) Etude — Miss K., 6 (72 73 74), 3 Chinese Etudes, 7 (75) Miss P., 8 (76) Miss P.

XIII   A. TAUB
   1 (77) Portrait of a Boy, 2 (78) Portrait of a Girl, 3 (79) Portrait of a Boy, 4 (80) Portrait of a Man, 5 (81) Boats, 6 (81) Seashore (copy from Klod Monst's picture), 7 (83) Cows, 8 (84) Twilight, 9 (85) Moses, 10 (85) Street in Vilno Ghetto.

XIV   MRS. R. ZIRULSKY-YANOVICH
   1 (87) Hanukka Candles, 2 (88) Old Jew, 3 (89) Portrait of Mr. Azar, 4 (90) Japanese Lady, 5 (91) Portrait of Artist Klem, 6 (92) Cut-Glass, 7 (93) Mr. Shvilli, 8 (94) Mr. Sirota, 9 (95) A Chinese in a fur cap, 10 (96) A Chinese, 11 (97) Flowers 12 (98) Landscape 13 (99) Anechka, 14 (100) Nadia, 15 (101) Fortune-Teller.

ABOVE LEFT: **Portrait of Semek Kushner, in pencil, by Yonia Fain.** Kushner's father and brother were killed in Shanghai near the end of the war during an American air raid on Japanese targets in Hongkew. *Yonia Fain, New York*

ABOVE RIGHT: **Portrait of Janek Goldstein, in pencil, by Yonia Fain.** The artist's friend in Shanghai, Goldstein was the son of Bernard Goldstein, who was active in the Bundist underground of the Warsaw ghetto and participated in the 1943 uprising. *Yonia Fain, New York*

LEFT: **Page from the catalogue of an exhibition of work by Jewish artists, held at the Shanghai Jewish Club, May 5–8, 1943.** Yonia Fain and A. Taub, whose pictures were included in the show, were Polish refugees. The other artists were refugees from Germany and Russian Jewish residents of Shanghai. *USHMM, Gift of Rebeka Ilutovich*

ABOVE: Rose Shoshana Kahan (center) and fellow refugee actors in the cast of Sholem Aleichem's Yiddish play *200,000,* performed in Shanghai on November 21, 1942. *Joseph Fiszman, Oregon*

RIGHT: Residents of the restricted area of Hongkew needed permission to exit to such places as the Shanghai Jewish Club, outside the ghetto. Operated by the Russian Jewish community, the club sponsored plays, lectures, and concerts and organized charitable events to benefit the refugees. *Joseph Fiszman, Oregon*

Shanghai Jewish Club
1623 AVENUE ROAD
Telephones 34205 (two lines)

Shanghai, 15th May 19 44.

To the
Shanghai Stateless Refugees Affairs Bureau,
70 Muirhead Road,
Shanghai.

Dear Sirs,

We shall be greatly obliged if you will grant a Special Pass good for 20 days to Mr.Joseph Fischman who is taking part in a Jewish Play scheduled to take place on the 10th June in the premises of our Club.

The required time for the Pass is from 10 a.m. to 9 p.m. for daily rehersals.

Thanking you in advance, we remain,

Yours faithfully,
SHANGHAI JEWISH CLUB
H. Kallman
President

husband reconstructed from memory. Many of Kahan's performances, as well as lectures and concerts, were held at the Shanghai Jewish Club, which was operated by the Russian Jewish community. After the establishment of the restricted area, theatrical productions and other cultural events became less frequent because the Polish Jewish performers were now separated from the Russian audience still free to live outside the area. The audience for such plays, mostly older Russian Jews, was also reduced.

Members of the Mir Yeshiva and other refugee yeshiva students in Shanghai spent the war years continuing their studies at the Beth Aharon Synagogue. The students spent part of each day listening to teachers lecture on Jewish Scripture and rabbinical commentaries. During the rest of the day, they paired up to review selections from the lecture. The yeshiva arranged to reprint

Students of the Beth Jacob School, Shanghai. Before the war, Chana Gorfinkel, the wife of a Mir Yeshiva student, had taught in Beth Jacob schools in Poland, which provided instruction in Hebrew and the Bible for Jewish girls. In Shanghai, she helped establish a branch of Beth Jacob. *Sarah Landesman, Maryland*

The Shanghai Jewish Youth Association School was established by local Jewish philanthropist Horace Kadoorie. A British citizen, Kadoorie insisted that classes be conducted in English, the working language of the International Settlement. *Beth Hatefutsoth Photo Archive, Israel*

religious texts for study and eventually published editions of the Bible and commentaries, the Talmud, various philosophical and religious tracts, as well as several original works.[50] The Russian Jewish community helped pay for the printing of books in Yiddish and Hebrew.

The yeshiva students' long daily trek to and from the ghetto became a familiar sight. "In fact, the sight of the yeshiva world, a serene island of scholarship in a sea of turbulent events made a strong impression on the refugees," one Mir student later recalled. "They themselves felt stimulated to stand more firmly in their Judaism."[51] The yeshiva established kosher kitchens where Passover matzah could be baked, and encouraged some Jewish stores to close on the Sabbath.

Religious education for younger refugees was also available in Shanghai. The student body of the Talmud Torah, an afternoon religious academy for boys, grew to over 300, and some of its students would join the Mir Yeshiva.[52] The Beth Jacob School for girls employed as teachers a number of women who had taught at Beth Jacob institutions in prewar Poland.[53]

Secular education took place at a number of schools, including the Shanghai Jewish Youth Association School, which predated the refugees' arrival in Shanghai and was supported by the Jewish philanthropist Horace Kadoorie. The "Kadoorie School" offered a stable routine for its student body of 600 and to a degree helped to shield the children from the more bitter hardships of exile. As a result, many would look back on their Shanghai adventure as an exciting time in an exotic place.[54] For older students, the Organization for Rehabilitation through Training (ORT) offered vocational training instruction in such fields as carpentry, bookbinding, and fashion design.

THE WAR AND GHETTO LIFE

As the war dragged on, life in Hongkew's restricted area and the deprivations of war took a toll on the refugees. In 1944, the Japanese curtailed the issuance of long-term exit passes as part of a campaign to force refugees to work full-time inside the ghetto. Food shortages and the constriction of employment forced more and more people to turn to the relief committees. The winter of 1943–1944 saw the ghetto's darkest days. In March, a Shanghai relief worker advised the Joint's New York office, "General condition in Shanghai here has become from bad to worse. Consequently, the number of destitutes is constantly increasing."[55]

Throughout the war, the Joint appealed to the U.S. government to abolish the restrictions that prevented the organization from transferring funds to Shanghai. Following Laura Margolis's repatriation in September 1943, she provided a firsthand account of the dire conditions in Shanghai. Together with the sympathetic receptiveness of Henry Morgenthau, secretary of the U.S. Treasury, this testimony proved decisive, and in March 1944 the Joint succeeded in sending $25,000 to Shanghai by way of Switzerland. The money arrived just in time to save thousands of refugees from starvation.[56] Members of the Mir Yeshiva survived this crisis more easily because Vaad ha-Hatzala had been channeling relief funds to them through neutral countries since the beginning of hostilities.[57]

After D-Day and the landings in Normandy, France, in June 1944, reports about the progress of the war gave the refugees cause for hope, as the tide gradually shifted in the Allies' favor. At the end of 1944, the tyrannical Japanese administrators of the pass system in the restricted area were replaced by more-evenhanded officials. The news of the German surrender in May 1945 roused optimistic expectations that Japan's

defeat was imminent. This feeling was rein-
forced by the appearance of American
bombers over Shanghai. But on July 17, 1945,
tragedy struck the ghetto. American aircraft
targeted a Japanese military radio station
that was in the center of the restricted area.
A local newspaper summed up the damages:
"There were instances of suffocation from
collapsed buildings, injuries from splinters,
and other injuries. . . . A bomb which ex-
ploded in the middle of Kunping Road created a crater deeper than the height of a
man." Some 250 refugees were casualties; of
the 31 who died, seven were Polish Jews.
Thousands of Chinese were dead or
wounded.[58]

WAR'S END

For the refugees, the last days of the war
were marked by rumor and confusion.

Prematurely, on August 10, according to one
refugee, "news of the Japanese capitulation
spread like wildfire."[59] Not until September 7
did the Japanese military formally surrender control of Shanghai to the Chinese
army.[60] Numbed by weeks of false rumors,
Ernest Heppner recalled, the refugees were
not really convinced of Allied victory until
they saw strange and unfamiliar vehicles—
American jeeps—cruising through the
streets of Shanghai.[61]

The end of the war changed the refugees'
circumstances dramatically. Leaving the
ghetto, some returned to their old apartments. Rationing ended, and food and
other goods began to flow into the stores.
Although the Joint's relief rolls numbered
almost 10,000 until December 1945, supplies
were finally abundant.[62] Headed by Manuel
Siegel, the Shanghai Joint cooperated with

Special "V" Issue

Shanghai, Friday, September 7, 1945 — English Supplement No. 133 ("Our Life" No. 204)

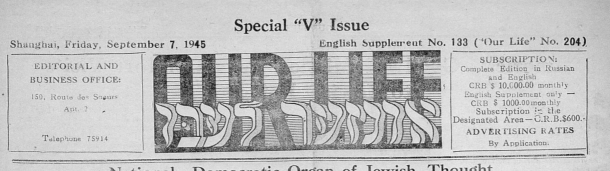

EDITORIAL AND BUSINESS OFFICE:

150, Route des Sœurs
Apt. 2

Telephone 75914

SUBSCRIPTION:
Complete Edition in Russian and English
CRB $ 10,000.00 monthly
English Supplement only —
CRB $ 1000.00 monthly
Subscription in the Designated Area—C.R.B.$600.-
ADVERTISING RATES
By Application.

National, Democratic Organ of Jewish Thought
Published Every Friday

Long Live Allied Victory!

The day has come when we, victims of Fascist aggression in Asia, can join our voice to that of the rest of our nation liberated by Allied victory from the death menace of Treblinkas and ghettos and cry out in boundless joy: we are saved!

We are saved, and our salvation is not only inseparably bound with Allied victory, it is part and parcel of it. All of us like one man knew that the alternative would be extinction and we have fought this war on the Allied side if not on the actual battlefield then in our hearts and minds. Six million Jewish victims who met their death not as gallant war heroes but in gas-cells and ghettos, is no mean contribution to the Allied cause, the contribution which the post-war world of Freedom and Justice will not be prone to minimize.

We say "The post-war world of Freedom and Justice", for we firmly believe that the world emerged out of the carnage and chaos of the past decade would have to be a much more decent and cleaner place for each man to live in. And in that world we, Jews, should win back our place of honour and dignity both as individuals and as a nation.

There is no doubt in our minds that we should be willing to become the most zealous architects of this future world, in ways big and small, knowing that we are building a solid abode for our children uninhabited by ghosts of hatred and prejudice that would scare them at night.

In the years gone by it was often said that Jewish children should not be born into the world that has no place for them and, perhaps, this cruel sentence was true. Their unborn souls have at least escaped the futile quest of the Blue Bird of Happiness so well depicted by Meterlinck. Let all those who have been born, however, not regret that a part of their lives was spent in the dark. "The darker was the night, the brighter will be stars", and still brighter the dazzling sun, the dawn of which we are welcoming at present.

It would be erroneous to expect, however, that heavenly mannah would be dropped for us from the clear skies without any effort on our part. To build the life on principles of equality, freedom and justice would require years of hard toil in all aphores of human endeavour; it would mean waging an ideological war against all remnants of poisonous doctrines implanted in the minds of thousands of people and preaching the new democratic gospel from all the pulpits and forums of the world.

It would be no exaggeration to say, however, that of all nations we, Jews, should form the most receptive audience for such a gospel. We are instinctively predisposed towards democratic principles which alone secure us, a weak minority, rights and freedom on a par with those nationals among whom we live. And whenever these principles are lacking, we are faced with restrictions of our most primitive rights, "Designated Areas", yellow armbands and other similar manifestations of inequality and exploitation.

The war that has just ended has retrieved for humanity its place in the twentieth century civilization which it had lost in the last decade. It recovered the human values trampled into the mud by wild Teutonic hordes.

And it has given Jews both as individuals and as a nation a new lease on life.

Long Live the Allied Victory!

Long live the peoples and leaders who have achieved it!

A. G.

"OUR LIFE"
Extends Heartfelt Felicitations
to its Friends and Readers
on occasion
of
ROSH HASHONO
and
"V" DAY

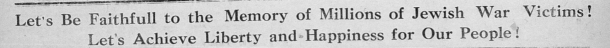

Let's Be Faithfull to the Memory of Millions of Jewish War Victims!
Let's Achieve Liberty and Happiness for Our People!

CHINA SERVICE COMMAND
IDENTIFICATION CARD

CIVILIAN EMPLOYEE

No. 817   Name Miss SONDHEIMER, HANNI

SECTION   SIGNAL

DATE OF ISSUE AUG 15 1945

CIVILIAN PERSONNEL OFFICER

the United Nations Relief and Rehabilitation Association to distribute food, blankets, and other provisions. American troops also offered supplies. Hanni Sondheimer Vogelweid remembered the day that U.S. Navy ships arrived, bearing undreamed-of delicacies. "We ate American ice cream for the first time and got kind of sick, it was so rich."[63] Hundreds of refugees, especially those who could speak English, found work with the American troops. By March 1946, the U.S. Armed Forces employed about 1,400 refugees in Shanghai.[64]

Few of the refugees wished to remain in Shanghai. But news of the Holocaust quelled any incentive to return to eastern Europe. With the Polish quota for U.S. immigration visas filled for years to come, most refugees headed to Australia, New Zealand, Mexico, Canada, or, after 1948, Israel. Most Mir students went to either Jerusalem or New York in 1946 and 1947, reestablishing the yeshiva at the two new locations. By 1949, with China in Communist hands, all but a tiny number of refugees had left Shanghai.

די אידישע שטימע

פון ווייטן מזרח

ארטאדאקסישע צייטשהיפט

| SHANGHAI, DECEMBER 1945 | № 1 | כ"ה שאנכיי, טבת תש"ו |

ב: מאנדלבוים

חורבן פולן

5.700.000

יזכור אלקים — געדענק ג-ט. מער בעטן מיר נישט.

געדענק בלויז אין די 5,700.000.

פינף מיליאן זיבן הונדערט טויזנט — עס בלוטיקט דאם הארץ. עם ציטערט די האנט אויפשרייבנדיק אזא ציפער.

דריי דורות האבן מיר פארלארן, דעם אלטן זיידן מיטן אייניקל. ביידע האט מען אין איין מאג געשחטן.

עם קלאגן די פעלדער פון פוילן, עם יאמערן די ביימער פון ליטע. עם וויינט דאם פארשאלטענע אייראפע — וואו זענען אונזערע יידן? פארוואס איז אונדזער ערד פאר זיי א קבר געווארן?

פון די טיפענישן פון דער ערד רייסט זיך נאך ארוים דאם קרעכצן פון דער מוטער, וואם איז לעבנדיק באגראבן געווארן צוזאמען מיט איר ניי-געבארן קינד.

ג-ט! אויב שווער איז פאר דיר די תפלה פון לע-בנדיקן ייד, מא דערהער דאם געבעט פון 5,700.000 וואם זענען מיט ליבשאפט פאר דיין נאמען פארברענט געווארן.

ג-ט! די הייליקע עדה פון טרעבלינקי בעטן רחמים פאר דיין פארשעמט פאלק ישראל.

ג-ט! די זוויג-קינדער פון בוכנוואלד שרייען טאטעניו.

טאטעניו, העכף שוין דיין צעבראבן פאלק ישראל.

און מיר, צעבראבענע שארבנם, טרוקענע סקעלעטן, רופן צו דיר: רבש"ע, צעריים דעם גזר-דין, גענוג שוין אונדזער ליידן. זאלן די קרבנות 5,700.000 נישט זיין אומזיסט.

יזכור אלקים...

ע. שמחוני.

וואס זענען אין די לעצטע 6 יאר פארגאנגען געווארן?!

די גויישע וועלט צײלט די קרבנות, וואם די פארניכטונג פון דער דייטשער טיראניע האט איר געקאסט. פיל זע-נען זיי. מיליאנען דערגרייכן זיי. אבער מיר האבן געצאלט דעם טייערסטן פרייז, קוואנטיטאטיוו און קוואליטאטיוו. דער פראבט און גלאנץ אין פון אונדז אוועקגענומען געווארן.

פארשוואונדן דאס פוילישע יידנטום! פארשוואונדן דער גייסטיקער אריסטא-קראט. אפגעהאקט געווארן דער רידערדע-דיקסטער, אימפולסיווסטער, ענערגישסטער גליד פון יידישן פאלקס-ארגאניזם. אוימגעטריקנט סאיז געפלאסן לעבנס-זאפט פארן גאנצן פאלק אין זיין גלות צע-שפרייטקייט.

נישטא מער די גדולי וצדיקי הדור, וואם האבן אונדז באלויבטן די פינס-טערע גלות-וועגן; וואם האבן אונדז געלערנט, ווי אזוי צו לעבן, ווי אזוי דאם ערדישע לעבן אין הימלישעם צו פאראווא נדלען; וואם האבן אונדזערע אינד א-כענם אין שבתים פארוואנ-דעלט, געווארימט אונדזערע הערצער, באשטראלט אונדזערע נשמות מיטן אור אין-סוף. נישטא מער דער ייד מיטן ברייטן טיף-צעצאקערטן לומדישן שטערן; דער הימליש-פארבענקטער און אין די אצילות-קוואלן געלייטערטער חסיד. נישטא מער דער פשוטער פאלקס-ייד, פון וועלט סהאט ארוייסגע-שטראלט אזיפל תמימות, הארציקייט און ליבשאפט צום גאנצן באשאף, אז מוחאלט דערמיט א האלבע גע-קענע פארטיילן.

און איצט — נישטא מער דאם אלף, ווים און לעער אויף די וועזני פון פוילן. פארשטומט געווארן די הימלישע סימפאניע, וואם די יידישע שטעט און שטעטלעך האבן הונדערטער יארן אויסגעזונגען.

און וויא צו פארטינען די טראנעדיע, ווי אומעיליבערער צו מאבן די וואונד, האבן די דייטשע בעסטיעם מיט וויל-דער אויסרעכענונג אפגענומען ביי אונדז די מעגלעכקייט אפילו צו קענען אויס-וויינען זיך ביים טיערסטע מצבה-שטיין. דאם עלעמענטארע מענטשלעכע רעכט אויף א איינגראבן ד' אמות אונדזערע קדושים נישט געגעבן געווארן. אויף שבעה ימים איז דאם אש פון זייערע היילינע קערפערס פאנאנדערגעשפרייט.

יא, עס איז די חרפה פון דער מענטש-ווערם אויער אזוי פיל רשעות ליים גע-

(ענדע אויף זייט 2)

נער ביים ארויסברענגען פון די פעדער די דאזיקע ווערטער. עם פירן די ווארצלען פון די האר אין דאם קאפ. טוי-זענט יאר יידיש לעבן און שפאן איז געווארן פארוואנדעלט אין רויכן אין אש. די דייטשע בלוט-הינט, די נאצי-שע קאניבאלן האבן זייער גאנצע רשעות און סאדים אריויסגעוויזן ביי דער פארניכטונג פון פוילישן יידנטום. די בעסטיעם האבן נישט געוואוסט פון קיין אפהאלט. טאג און נאכט האבן געפלאקערט די מעדירנע קאלך-אויוונס און פארצערט דאם טיערסטע שענסטע און אומפארשעצבארסטע, וואם מיר האבן פארמאגט: די ימים יידישע בלוט און טרערן. אריומאנט — 6 יאר מלחמה — 6 עקידה.

וואם דאם פוילישע יידנטום:

ווען מיר שרייבן וועגן חורבן-פוילן, מיינען מיר, נאטירלעך, דעם חורבן פון יידישן פוילן, פונם פוילן, וואם איז געווען דאם שווארצאפל, דאם יכט פון אונדזערע אויגן. ווייל אויב י' יהודה הלוי ז"ל זאגט ערגעץ, אז דען זענען דאם הארץ פון דער וועלט, אן מען זיכערלעך צוגעבן, אז דאם יידישע יידנטום איז געווען דאם ארץ, דער באפרוטספערונדיקער קואל, דער קדשי-קדשים פון יידישן פאלק.

וואם איז פאר אונדז דאם פוילישע יידנטום געווען? אלק. אלץ וואם האט דאם יידישע פאלק געקענטען ביים גייסטיק ייכן יידיש-פוילישן קיבוץ. תורה. כמה, לומדות, חסידות, מוסר — אלק, אן מען נאר געהאטן א שייכות מיטן יידישן גייסט האט געצויגן זיין יניקה אין זיין שוים איז געווארן וויסגעווארימט די דערהויבנבסטע אי-עאלן, די שענסטע ווערטן פון יידישן אלקס-אוצר. אין פוילן האט מען גע-עם, און וואם אזוינס סאיז די לעבן, און וואם אזוינס איז מיין ייד זיי. דארט אט מען מיט די הענט געקענט אן-אפן קדושה וטהרה. וועמען דער אוי-ערשטער האט געבענטשט מיט טיפע פ ורכדרינגענדע אויגן, האט פון די טומע ברוק-שטיינער געקענט אראפ-ענגען, אז אויף זיי האט א ייד גע-ראטן. דרייסיק דורות יידן אין פוילן זיינען מסירת-נפש פאר דריסיק דורות פאטענטין און אדלער-פלי צו דעם עקסטע האריזאנטעם פון יידישער לעטור, פון מקורות יידישן יידיש וויסן.

און איצט — ווי, ווי, — חורבן ווילן! דער קאף, ווי אנגעגאסן מיט לייי, העכף מיר אויף צו טראכטן. דאם הענטעל ווערט אטארשיפעל. ווי העכף זיך מאכטלאם אראפ. אוי, רבש"ע הי' לנו! נישט אין קיין טינט, נאר אין ימים זודיק בלוט פון מיליאנען רושים וועירט היינט געטונקען אונזער עדער. און גראד אונדזער דור אין עם באשערט אויף זיינע שוואכע פליי-גנס-לאסטן. און נישט איינמאל, אין אמענטן פון דערדריקנדיקן צער, ען דאם הארץ קורטשעט זיך פון פיין ון ליידער, וויל זיך אויסשרייען מיט ווערטער פון ירמיה: אוי לי אמי כי דתני! אז אך און ווייי איז צו אונדז וואבן געבליבענע. אנה אנו באם, וואו וועלן מיר זיך ווינקל, וואו וועלן מיר געפינען א ווינקל, וואם זאל אונדז דערימען וואם איז אונדז חורבן פוילן?!

נישטא מער דאם פוילישע יידנטום!

REMEMBRANCE

The joy of liberation gave way to despair and disbelief as reports of the systematic annihilation of Europe's Jewry reached the refugees. Each day, they scanned the lists of survivors posted by Jewish newspapers and the International Red Cross. The happiness upon learning that a loved one was still alive was quickly muted by the realization that millions of others had died.[1] Detailed reports of the atrocities were printed in the Jewish newspapers, including descriptions of the killing centers at Treblinka and Auschwitz. The scope of the tragedy was impossible to comprehend. "We found out, we couldn't believe it, but we found out," lamented one refugee.[2]

The murder of millions of Jews in Europe accentuated in the minds of many refugees how extraordinarily fortunate they were to be alive. Approximately six million Jews perished in the Holocaust; three million of them were Polish. Rose Shoshana Kahan wrote in her diary: "We Polish refugees go around with tear-stained faces because we left everybody on the other side. Many feel guilty that they survived, when their loved ones died a terrible death."[3]

The photographs that follow were saved by refugees who escaped to Japan and points beyond. Some photographs show these survivors with loved ones in prewar Poland.

GOD REMEMBER—GOD REMEMBER; WE DO NOT ASK FOR MORE.

JUST REMEMBER THE 5,700,000.

FIVE MILLION SEVEN HUNDRED THOUSAND—THE HEART BLEEDS,

THE HAND TREMBLES WHEN WRITING DOWN SUCH A NUMBER.

THREE GENERATIONS WE HAVE LOST, THE OLD GRANDFATHER

WITH HIS GRANDCHILD. BOTH WERE SLAUGHTERED ON THE SAME

DAY. THE FIELDS OF POLAND LAMENT, THE TREES OF LITHUANIA

WEEP, AND CURSED EUROPE IS CRYING—WHERE ARE

OUR JEWS? WHY DID OUR EARTH BECOME

A GRAVE FOR THEM?

TIMELINE

SEPTEMBER 1, 1939
Germany invades Poland.

SEPTEMBER 17, 1939
The Soviet Union invades Poland from the east.

SEPTEMBER 28, 1939
Poland is partitioned by the Soviet Union and Germany in accordance with the German-Soviet Non-Aggression Pact (Ribbentrop-Molotov Accord).

OCTOBER 11, 1939
The American Jewish Joint Distribution Committee begins relief activity in Lithuania. American social worker Moses Beckelman directs operations from Vilna.

OCTOBER 28, 1939
Vilna and its environs are transferred from Soviet to Lithuanian control. From September 1939 through early 1940, more than 15,000 Polish Jews flee to Lithuania, mostly to Vilna, to escape Nazi persecution and Soviet domination.

NOVEMBER 23, 1939
The Nazis introduce the Jewish Star of David as an identifying badge in German-occupied Poland.

APRIL 30, 1940
The Germans seal the first major ghetto confining Jews in Lodz, Poland. Jews from Polish territories incorporated into the Reich are deported there.

MAY 10, 1940
Germany invades Belgium, Luxembourg, and the Netherlands.

JUNE 14, 1940
German troops enter Paris.

JUNE 15, 1940
Soviet troops invade Lithuania.

JUNE 19, 1940
The Dutch ambassador in Riga, Latvia, L. P. J. de Decker, notifies the Dutch Foreign Ministry-in-exile in London of his appointment of Jan Zwartendijk, director of Lithuanian operations for the Dutch company Philips, as acting consul for Lithuania.

JULY 22—AUGUST 2, 1940
Acting on de Decker's authorization, Zwartendijk issues bogus destination visas for entry into the Dutch West Indies. Zwartendijk's operation is shut down when the Soviets seize his Philips office as part of a large nationalization campaign.

JULY 11—AUGUST 31, 1940
The Japanese acting consul to Lithuania, Chiune Sugihara, issues more than 2,100 transit visas, mostly to Polish Jewish refugees holding Zwartendijk visas.

AUGUST 4, 1940
The USSR officially annexes Lithuania and orders all diplomatic consulates in Kaunas to close by August 25, 1940 (later extended to September 4).

AUGUST 16, 1940
The first small groups of refugees begin arriving in Japan. A few hundred will arrive by the end of 1940.

SEPTEMBER 4, 1940
Japan closes its consulate in Kaunas, Lithuania. Sugihara leaves Lithuania for Berlin en route to his new post in Prague.

SEPTEMBER 1940
Zwartendijk returns to Philips headquarters in Eindhoven, German-occupied Netherlands.

OCTOBER 6, 1940
Laurence Steinhardt, U.S. ambassador to the Soviet Union, alerts Washington from Moscow of the more than 2,000 Japanese visas recently issued in Kaunas for transit en route

to the Dutch possessions in the Americas and expresses his concern that the real intention of the visa recipients is to enter the United States.

NOVEMBER 15, 1940
The Warsaw ghetto is sealed. In both size and population, it is the largest ghetto established by the Nazis. More than 350,000 Jews, about 30 percent of the city's population, are confined to less than 2.5 percent of the city's total area.

JANUARY 1, 1941
The Soviet Union orders all refugees in Lithuania to declare Soviet citizenship by January 25. The implicit punishment for failure to do so is exile to Siberia.

JANUARY–FEBRUARY 1941
Hundreds of Polish-Jewish refugees, most with Sugihara and Zwartendijk visas, leave Lithuania, cross the Soviet Union via the Trans-Siberian Railroad, and begin arriving in Japan.

FEBRUARY 28, 1941
In response to a request from the Japanese Foreign Ministry, Sugihara sends a list from Prague giving the names of 2,140 persons to whom he issued transit visas from Lithuania.

MAY 1941
In an exhibition titled *Wandering Jew* at the Osaka Asahi Kaikan, members of the avant-garde Tanpei Photography Club present their photographs of Polish Jewish refugees in Kobe.

JUNE 22, 1941
German forces invade the Soviet Union in the massive Operation Barbarossa. Mass shootings of Jews by Nazis and their collaborators begin in Lithuania.

AUGUST 31, 1941
The Nazis establish a ghetto in Vilna.

FALL 1941
In preparation for war, Japan expels nearly 1,000 Polish Jewish refugees stranded in Kobe, sending them to Shanghai, China, then under Japanese control.

DECEMBER 7, 1941
Japanese planes attack U.S. ships at Pearl Harbor, Hawaii.

DECEMBER 8, 1941
The Nazi killing center at Chelmno, northwest of Lodz, Poland, begins gassing operations. The United States declares war on Japan.

DECEMBER 11, 1941
Germany declares war on the United States.

JANUARY 20, 1942
German government leaders meet at the Wannsee Conference to discuss the implementation of the "Final Solution."

MARCH 17, 1942
The Belzec killing center in occupied Poland begins operations.

MAY 1942
The Sobibor killing center in occupied Poland begins gassing operations.

JULY 15, 1942
Deportations begin of Jews from the Netherlands to Auschwitz and Sobibor.

JULY 22– SEPTEMBER 21, 1942
Mass deportations from the Warsaw ghetto begin; approximately 265,000 Jews are killed at Treblinka.

FEBRUARY 18, 1943
Japanese authorities in Shanghai order all "stateless refugees," including Jewish refugees from Poland, Lithuania, Germany, and Austria, into a "designated area."

APRIL 19–MAY 16, 1943
The Warsaw ghetto revolt takes place. It ends with the destruction of the ghetto.

JUNE 6, 1944
D-Day: The Allied invasion of western Europe begins.

MAY 7, 1945
Allied troops declare victory in Europe.

AUGUST 14, 1945
Allied troops declare victory in Japan.

1947
Chiune Sugihara returns to U.S.-occupied Japan and is retired from the Japanese Foreign Ministry during restructuring under the occupation.

Owing to the lack of funds, visas, and available transport, most refugees do not leave Shanghai until 1947.

NOTES

Introduction

1. Karl A. Schleunes, "Emigration: Signpost to the Future," *The Twisted Road to Auschwitz: Nazi Policy toward German Jews, 1933–1939* (Urbana and Chicago: University of Illinois Press, 1990), 169–213; Leni Yahil, "Emigration: The Dilemma of the Jews (Through September 1, 1939)," in *The Holocaust: The Fate of European Jewry* (New York: Oxford University Press, 1990), 88–122.

2. American Jewish Joint Distribution Committee, "Aiding Jews Overseas: Report of the American Jewish Joint Distribution Committee, Inc. for 1940 and the first 5 months of 1941," June 26, 1941, 5–52, American Jewish Joint Distribution Committee Archives, New York City (hereafter AJJDC Archives), AR 33/44, file #157; *A Tale of Two Worlds*, American Jewish Joint Distribution Committee, 24 min., 1941, videocassette, National Center for Jewish Film, Brandeis University, Waltham, Mass.; Yehuda Bauer, *American Jewry and the Holocaust: The American Jewish Joint Distribution Committee, 1933–1945* (Detroit: Wayne State University Press, 1981) .

3. Dov Levin, *The Lesser of Two Evils: Eastern European Jewry under Soviet Rule, 1939–1941*, trans. Naftali Greenwood (Philadelphia: The Jewish Publication Society, 1995); Keith Sword, "The Mass Movement of Poles to the USSR, 1939–41," in *Deportation and Exile: Poles in the Soviet Union, 1939–48* (New York: St. Martin's Press, 1994), 1–27; Menachem Begin, *White Nights: The Story of a Prisoner in Russia* (New York: Harper & Row, 1957, 1977), 9–39; NKVD arrest and interrogation files of Menachem Begin, Morduch Bernsztejn, Jona Brumberg, Yossel Galperin, Lev Garfunkel, Perez Guterman, David Krol, Leon Oler, Miron Sheskin, Borel Vinokur, Brone Vinokur, Extraordinary Archive of Lithuania, Vilnius.

4. Raul Hilberg, "Statistics of Jewish Dead," in *The Destruction of the European Jews*, 3 vols. (New York: Holmes & Meier Publishers, Inc., 1985), 3:1201–20.

5. David S. Wyman, *Paper Walls: America and the Refugee Crisis 1938–1941* (Amherst: University of Massachusetts Press, 1968). The American response has also been discussed in Henry L. Feingold, *The Politics of Rescue: The Roosevelt Administration and the Holocaust, 1938–1945* (New York: Holocaust Library, 1970), and Richard Breitman and Alan M. Kraut, *American Refugee Policy and European Jewry, 1933–1945* (Bloomington: Indiana University Press, 1987).

6. Dorothy Thompson, *Refugees: Anarchy or Organization?* (New York: Random House, 1938), 28.

7. David Kranzler, "The Gates Close: Restrictions Go into Effect," in *Japanese, Nazis & Jews: The Jewish Refugee Community of Shanghai, 1938–1945* (Hoboken, N. J.: KTAV Publishing House, Inc., 1988), 267–80.

8. United States Holocaust Memorial Museum (hereafter USHMM), *Hidden History of the Kovno Ghetto* (Boston: Bulfinch Press, 1997).

9. Zorach Warhaftig, *Refugee and Survivor: Rescue Efforts during the Holocaust*, trans. Avner Tomaschoff (Jerusalem: Yad Vashem, 1988), 104.

Chapter 1: Flight

1. Markus Nowogrodzki, videotape interview, June 7, 1999, USHMM, Oral History, RG 50.494, #0002; Zorach Warhaftig, *Refugee and Survivor*, 33.

2. Susan Bluman, videotape interview, July 12, 1999, USHMM, Oral History, RG 50.494, #0015.

3. Wanda Glass, telephone interview with Clare Cronin of USHMM, September 17, 1998.

4. Yisrael Gutman, *Jews of Warsaw, 1939–1943: Ghetto, Underground, Revolt* (Bloomington: Indiana University Press, 1982), 8.

5. "Bulletin #4—War Relief Activities of JDC," American Joint Distribution Committee Report, November 9, 1939, USHMM, Archives, Records of the Jewish Labor Committee, Wagner Labor Archive, accession no. 1996.A.0586, microfilm reel 15, pp. 56–60.

6. Ruth Berkowicz Segal, videotape interview, August 3, 1999, USHMM, Oral History, RG 50.494, #0016

7. Bluman, interview.

8. Chaya Lifshitz Waxman, "A Place Called Suwalk" (unpublished memoir, n.d.), 37–42, Chaya Waxman Private Collection.

9. Warhaftig, *Refugee and Survivor*, 28, 36–37.

10. *Encyclopedia of the Holocaust*, ed. Israel Gutman, 4 vols., s.v. "Poland" (New York: Macmillan Publishing Co., 1990), 3:1155.

11. "The Jewish Refugees in the Russian-Occupied Territory of Poland and in Lithuania. Report of Dr. M. Kleinbaum," in A. Hartglas et al., *Tragedy of Polish Jewry* (Jerusalem: Joint Committee for the Aid of the Jews of Poland, 1940), 46.

12. "The Jewish Refugees in the Russian-Occupied Territory of Poland and in Lithuania. Report of Dr. K. Schwartz," in Hartglas et al., *Tragedy of Polish Jewry*, 56.

13. Moshe Kleinbaum (Geneva) to Nahum Goldman, March 12, 1940, "The Papers of the World Jewish Congress, 1939–1945," in *Archives of the Holocaust*, vol. 8, ed. Abraham J. Peck (New York and London: Garland Publishing, Inc., 1990), 107–9.

14. Josef Rotenberg, *Fun Varshe biz Shangkhay: notitsn fun a polet* (From Warsaw to Shanghai: Notes of a Refugee) (Mexico: Shelomoh Mendelson-fond bay der gezelshaft far kultur un hilf, 1948), 137.

15. Alexander Schenker, videotape interview, June 22, 1999, USHMM, Oral History, RG 50.494, #0009.

16. Moses W. Beckelman, Report for Joint Distribution

Committee, February 1940, AJJDC Archives, AR 33/44, file #730 (1937–1950).

17. Yitzhak Arad, "Concentration of Refugees in Vilna on the Eve of the Holocaust," *Yad Vashem Studies on the European Jewish Catastrophe and Resistance* 9, ed. Livia Rothkirchen (1973): 207; Yitzhak Arad, *Ghetto in Flames: The Struggle and Destruction of the Jews in Vilna in the Holocaust* (New York: Holocaust Library, 1982), 11; Bauer, *American Jewry and the Holocaust,* 108.

18. Yehuda Bauer, "Rescue Operations through Vilna," *Yad Vashem Studies on the European Jewish Catastrophe and Resistance* 9 (1973): 215.

19. Chana Giterman Frydman, interview with Susan Bachrach of USHMM, October 23, 1998, New York, N.Y.

20. Warhaftig, *Refugee and Survivor,* 40.

21. Leo Melamed, videotape interview, June 12, 1999, USHMM, Oral History, RG 50.494, #0006.

22. Norbert Swislocki, videotape interview, June 23, 1999, USHMM, Oral History, RG 50.494, #0011.

23. Ruzhe Shoshano Kahan (Rose Shoshana Kahan), *In Fayer un Flamen: toghukh fun a Yidisher shoyshpilern* (In Fire and Flames: Diary of a Yiddish Actress) (Buenos Aires: Tsentralfarband fun Poylishe Yiden in Argentina, 1949), diary entry of January 15, 1940, 246.

24. For a discussion of the waves of immigration to Vilna, see Arad, "Concentration of Refugees," 201–14.

25. Ibid., 206.

26. Bernard Weinryb, "Polish Jews under Soviet Rule," in *The Jews in the Soviet Satellites,* ed. Peter Meyer, Bernard D. Weinryb, Eugene Duschinsky, and Nicholas Sylvain (Westport, Conn.: Greenwood Press, 1953, 1971), 342.

27. Bianca Sztejn Lloyd, telephone interview with Paul Rose of USHMM, September 16, 1998.

28. Hirsch Kupinsky, telephone interview with Paul Rose of USHMM, July 23, 1998.

29. Shmuel (Samuel) Soltz, *Eight Hundred and Fifty Days from Border to Border during the Second World War* (Givatayim, Israel: Shmuel Soltz, 1988), 55.

Chapter 2: Refuge

1. Moses W. Beckelman, "The Refugee Problem in Lithuania," February 1940, AJJDC Archives, AR 33/44, #730 (1937–1950).

2. Ibid.

3. For statistics, see Bauer, "Rescue Operations through Vilna," 215; Warhaftig, *Refugee and Survivor,* 42; Beckelman, "Refugee Problem."

4. Efraim Zuroff, *The Response of Orthodox Jewry in the United States to the Holocaust: The Activities of the Vaad ha-Hatzala Rescue Committee, 1939–1945* (New York: Michael Scharf Publication Trust of the Yeshiva University Press, 2000), 23–26.

5. Ibid.; Rabbi Yitzchak Kasnett, *The World That Was: Lithuania* (Cleveland Heights, Ohio: Hebrew Academy of Cleveland, 1996), 37.

6. Samuel Schmidt to his wife, March 17, 1940, American Jewish Archives, Cincinnati, Ohio, Schmidt Collection.

7. Moses Beckelman, "Lithuania," December 1939, AJJDC Archives, AR 33/44, #730.

8. Bernard Gufler to Cordell Hull, April 4, 1940, National Archives and Records Administration, Washington, D.C. (hereafter NARA), RG 59, 860M.4016/39.

9. Beckelman, "Lithuania."

10. Kleinbaum, "The Jewish Refugees," 53.

11. Arad, "Concentration of Refugees," 207; Arad, *Ghetto in Flames,* 11; Bauer, *American Jewry and the Holocaust,* 108.

12. Owen J. C. Norem to Cordell Hull, November 10, 1939, NARA, RG 59, lot 52D408, Records of the Intergovernmental Committee on Refugees (ICR), country file "Lithuania."

13. Gufler to Hull, April 4, 1940.

14. Kleinbaum, "The Jewish Refugees," Appendix.

15. Bluman, interview; Markus Nowogrodzki, interview; Meri Nowogrodzki, videotape interview, June 7, 1999, USHMM, Oral History, RG 50.494, #0001.

16. Kahan, *In Fayer un Flamen,* diary entry of January 30, 1940, 247.

17. Melamed, interview.

18. Hanni Sondheimer Vogelweid, videotape interview, July 8, 1999, USHMM, Oral History, RG 50.494, #0013.

19. Soltz, *Eight Hundred and Fifty Days,* 58.

20. Yitzhak Giterman, budget, November and December 1939, AJJDC Archives, AR 33/44, #730.

21. Bulletin #4—"War Relief Activities of the JDC," November 9, 1939.

22. Bauer, "Rescue Operations," 217; Moses Beckelman, statement to the press, May 21, 1941, AJJDC Archives, AR 33/44, #732.

23. Schmidt to his wife, March 17, 1940.

24. Henrietta K. Buchman, "Distribution of Funds in Lithuania" (memorandum to JDC), May 22, 1940, AJJDC Archives, AR 33/44, #730; Beckelman, "Lithuania"; Beckelman, "Refugee Problem."

25. Beckelman, "Refugee Problem"; Z. Zarecki, "Activities Report of the Refugee Relief Committee of the Kehillah in Vilnius for January 1940," AJJDC Archives, AR 33/44, #730.

26. Beckelman, "Refugee Problem."

27. Ibid.

28. Ibid.

29. Soltz, *Eight Hundred and Fifty Days,* 59.

30. Warhaftig, *Refugee and Survivor,* 46.

31. Ibid.; Beckelman, "Refugee Problem."

32. "Moshe Kleinbaum's Report on Issues in the Former Eastern Polish Territories, March 12, 1940," in *Jews in Eastern Poland and the USSR, 1939–46,* ed. Norman Davis and Antony Polonsky (New York: St. Martin's Press, 1991), 287.

33. Rotenberg, *Fun Varshe biz Shangkhay,* 232.

34. Markus Nowogrodzki, interview.

35. Bluman, interview.

36. Beckelman, "Lithuania."

37. JDC Paris to JDC New York, regarding reports from Beckelman, March 1, 1940, AJJDC Archives, AR 33/44, #730.

38. Beckelman, "Refugee Problem."

39. Ibid.

40. Zarecki, "Activities Report."

41. Warhaftig, *Refugee and Survivor*, 52.

42. Zuroff, *Response of Orthodox Jewry*, 26–40.

43. "Decree of the Commissioner for War Refugees," December 21, 1939, enclosed in Bernard Gufler to Cordell Hull, February 13, 1940, NARA, RG 59, lot 52D408, Records of the ICR, country file "Lithuania."

44. Zarecki, "Activities Report"; Bernard Gufler to Cordell Hull, January 8, 1940, NARA, RG 165, G-2 regional file "Lithuania," box 2407.

45. Zarecki, "Activities Report."

46. Arad, "Concentration of Refugees," 209.

47. Beckelman, "Refugee Problem."

48. Zarecki, "Activities Report."

49. Chaim Lipschitz, *The Shanghai Connection* (New York: Maznaim Publishing Co., 1988), 22.

50. Soltz, *Eight Hundred and Fifty Days*, 64–66.

51. Warhaftig, *Refugee and Survivor*, 45.

52. Bluman, interview.

53. Moses Beckelman to JDC Paris, May 9, 1940, AJJDC Archives, AR 33/44, #730; Zuroff, "Rescue via the Far East," 160, citing JDC figures.

54. Zarecki, "Activities Report."

55. Bernard Gufler to Cordell Hull, February 17, 1940, NARA, RG 59, Records of the ICR, country file "Lithuania."

56. Arad, "Concentration of Refugees," 209; Bauer, *American Jewry and the Holocaust*, 114; Beckelman, "Refugee Problem."

57. Beckelman, "Refugee Problem."

58. "Decree of the Commissar for the Care of War Refugees," January 18, 1940, enclosed in Moses Beckelman to M. C. Troper, February 17, 1940, AJJDC Archives, AR 33/44, #730.

59. Ibid.

60. Rotenberg, *Fun Varshe biz Shangkhay*, 250.

61. "Verordnungsblatt des Generalgouvernements für die besetzten polnischen Gebiete" (Decree on identification of Jewish men and women in the General Government), November 23, 1939, in Yitzhak Arad, *Documents on the Holocaust* (Lincoln: University of Nebraska Press, 1999; Jerusalem: Yad Vashem, 1999), 178–79.

62. Beckelman, "Refugee Problem."

63. Meri Nowogrodzki, interview.

64. Rotenberg, *Fun Varshe biz Shangkhay*, 250.

65. Warhaftig, *Refugee and Survivor*, 85.

66. Beckelman, "Refugee Problem."

67. Rotenberg, *Fun Varshe biz Shangkhay*, 238.

68. Lucille Szepsenwol Camhi, videotape interview, June 8, 1999, USHMM, Oral History, RG 50.494, #0003.

69. "Kleinbaum's Report, March 12, 1940," 287.

70. Ibid.

71. Ibid.

72. Rotenberg, *Fun Varshe biz Shangkhay*, 230.

73. Meri Nowogrodzki, interview.

74. Melamed, interview.

75. Kahan, *In Fayer un Flamen*, diary entry of December 8, 1939, 243.

76. Ibid., diary entry of March 17, 1940, 249.

77. Rotenberg, *Fun Varshe biz Shangkhay*, 234.

78. Schmidt to his wife, December 25, 1940.

79. Swislocki, interview.

MIR YESHIVA:
Zuroff, *Response of Orthodox Jewry*, passim; Lipschitz, *Shanghai Connection*, passim.

MOSES BECKELMAN:
AJJDC Archives, Moses Beckelman biographical file, #123B.

ZORACH WARHAFTIG:
Warhaftig, *Refugee and Survivor*, passim.

Chapter 3: Soviet Takeover

1. Camhi, interview.

2. Alex Shtromas, "Soviet Occupation of the Baltic States and Their Incorporation into the USSR: Political and Legal Aspects," *East European Quarterly* 14, no. 3 (September 1985): 289–301.

3. Owen J. C. Norem to Cordell Hull, July 25, 1940, NARA, microfilm, M-1178, RG 59, 860M.00/457.

4. Arad, *Ghetto in Flames*, 21. The official exchange rate of 5.9 litas to the dollar is used here.

5. Vogelweid, interview.

6. Gufler to Hull, April 4, 1940.

7. Bauer, *American Jewry and the Holocaust*, 117.

8. Arad, *Ghetto in Flames*, 22.

9. Kahan, *In Fayer un Flamen*, diary entry of September 28, 1940, 254.

10. Bernard Gufler to Cordell Hull, August 29, 1940, NARA, microfilm, M1284, RG 59, "Calamities," 840.48/4207.

11. Giersz Bider, "Meeting of the Executive Committee (The present situation in Lithuania)" (report for Joint Distribution Committee), November 27, 1940, AJJDC Archives, AR 33/44, #732.

12. Bauer, "Rescue Operations through Vilna," 219.

13. Bider, "Meeting of the Executive Committee."

14. Zorach Warhaftig and Eliezer Szczupakiewicz (Kobe, Japan) to JDC New York, November 19, 1940, AJJDC Archives, AR 33/44, #723.

15. Norem to Hull, July 25, 1940.

16. Warhaftig, *Refugee and Survivor*, 93.

17. *Contemporary Jewish Record: Review of Events and Digest of Opinion* (New York: American Jewish Committee, September–October 1940), 541.

18. Soltz, *Eight Hundred and Fifty Days*, 68.

19. Camhi, interview.

20. Begin, *White Nights*, 53ff.

21. American Representation of General Jewish Workers Union of Poland, *The Case of Henryk Erlich and Victor Alter* (New York: American Representation of General Jewish Workers Union of Poland, 1943); Lukasz Hirszowicz, "NKVD Documents Shed New Light on Fate of Erlich and Alter," *East European Jewish Affairs* 22, no. 2 (Winter 1992): 65–85.

22. Melamed, interview.

23. Soltz, *Eight Hundred and Fifty Days*, 67.

1. Warhaftig, *Refugee and Survivor,* 104.

2. Laurence Steinhardt, U.S. Ambassador to the Soviet Union, to Cordell Hull, October 31, 1940, NARA, RG 59, General Records of the U.S. Department of State, Visa Division, 811.111, "Refugees," 636.

3. Warhaftig, *Refugee and Survivor,* 73, 139. Warhaftig mentions two different prices for the "safe conduct" certificates: 300 and 350 litas. In some instances, yeshiva students were able to obtain these papers at a reduced rate of 100 litas—still beyond the reach of the students, who received no more than 13 litas every week.

4. Ibid., 89–90, 95–97.

5. *Statutes at Large of the United States of America from December 1923 to March 1925* (Washington, D.C.: United States Government Printing Office, 1925), vol. 42, part 1, 153.

6. *The Department of State Bulletin* (Washington, D.C.: United States Government Printing Office, 1940), vol. 3, 563; *Foreign Relations of the United States* (Washington, D.C.: United States Government Printing Office, 1957), vol. 2, 236; Breckinridge Long to Franklin D. Roosevelt, Library of Congress, Washington, D.C., Breckinridge Long Papers, box 5.

7. Bernard Gufler to Department of State, September 2, 1940, NARA, RG 59, 811.111/230, "Refugees."

8. Isaac Lewin, *Remember the Days of Old: Historical Essays* (New York: Research Institute of Religious Jewry, Inc., 1994), 174–75.

9. Lewin "safe conduct" document, Nathan Lewin Private Collection.

10. Jan Zwartendyk, Jr., videotape interview, July 7, 1999, USHMM, Oral History, RG 50.494, #0014. De Decker informed the Dutch Foreign Ministry-in-exile of Zwartendijk's appointment on June 19. Jan Zwartendyk, Jr., recalls that his father became acting consul approximately one day before the Soviet invasion, around June 14.

11. Jan Zwartendyk to Ministry of Foreign Affairs, The Hague, April 9, 1963, Netherlands Ministry of Foreign Affairs Archives, The Hague, file 153.3, "Zwartendijk."

12. The distance from Vilna to Kaunas is about 60 miles.

13. Lloyd, interview.

14. Warhaftig, *Refugee and Survivor,* 110.

15. L. P. J. de Decker, Personnel files, Netherlands Ministry of Foreign Affairs Archives, The Hague; Zwartendyk, interview.

16. A. M. de Jong to Shmuel Orlanski, August 11, 1966, Yad Vashem Archives, Jerusalem, file 03/3038.

17. Ibid.

18. Zwartendijk to Ministry of Foreign Affairs, April 9, 1963.

19. Zorach Warhaftig, interview with Dov Levin, November 30, 1965, Yad Vashem Archives, Jerusalem, Department for the Righteous, file 2861, "Sempo Sugihara."

20. Chiune Sugihara, unpublished report on his activities in Kaunas, 1939–1940, Yad Vashem Archives, Jerusalem, Department for the Righteous, file 2861, "Sempo Sugihara."

21. Cited in Ewa Palasz-Rutkowska and Andrzej T. Romer, "Polish-Japanese Co-operation during World War II," *Japan Forum* 7, no. 2 (Autumn 1995): 290, from an unpublished 1948 account by Leszek Daszkiewicz; Intelligence Report, "Centralia," September 24, 1940, Pilsudski Institute of America, Kasimierz Sosnowski Collection, I. file V (2), 161–62; Diagram of Polish Intelligence Network, July 29, 1940, Pilsudski Institute of America, Kasimierz Sosnowski Collection, I. file IV (2), 260.

22. Sugihara, unpublished report.

23. Chiune Sugihara to Foreign Minister Yosuke Matsuoka, cable #22785/#50, July 28, 1940, Japanese Foreign Ministry Diplomatic Record Office, Tokyo (hereafter JFMDRO), "Jewish Problem" file (hereafter JPF), I-4-6-0.1-2, folder 10.

24. Warhaftig, *Refugee and Survivor,* 106–7. See also Japanese transit visas issued in 1940 by the consulate in Kaunas ("Sugihara list"), which indicate the fee charged: JFMDRO, file J 2.3.0. J/X 2-6.

25. Sugihara, unpublished report.

26. Zwartendijk to Ministry of Foreign Affairs, The Hague, April 9, 1963.

27. "Sugihara list," July 30, 1940, JFMDRO, file J 2.3.0. J/X 2-6.

28. Moshe Zupnik, videotape interview, June 16, 1999, USHMM, Oral History, RG 50.494, #0007.

29. Tadeusz Romer, report of February 6, 1941, Tokyo, Hoover Institution Archives, Stanford, Calif., "Poland," M.S.Z. Collection, box 526, folder 7, "Refugees," 1941.

30. Sugihara to Matsuoka, July 28, 1940.

31. Foreign Minister Yosuke Matsuoka to Chiune Sugihara, cable #27465/#22, August 16, 1940, JFMDRO, JPF, folder 10; see also the cables from Matsuoka to Sugihara, #26848/#18, August 12, 1940; #27136/#21, August 14, 1940; #28710/#23, August 28, 1940.

32. Notation on Japanese transit visa issued by Chiune Sugihara to Bianca Sztejn Lloyd, August 31, 1940, USHMM Collection, Gift of Bianca Lloyd.

33. Chiune Sugihara to Foreign Minister Yosuke Matsuoka, cable #26809/#67, probably September 1, 1940 (misdated August 1; cable arrived in Tokyo on September 2, suggesting a typographical error), JFMDRO, folder 10.

34. Foreign Minister Yosuke Matsuoka to Chiune Sugihara, cable #29345/#24, September 3, 1940, JFMDRO, JPF, folder 10; Chiune Sugihara to Tokyo, September 6, 1940, NARA, RG 457, Entry 9011, SRDJ No. 006362, "Japanese Diplomatic Intercept Cables."

35. Lloyd, interview. The Sztejns received their second visas from Sugihara on August 31, 1940, although these do not appear on the list.

36. Sugihara (Prague) to American Division, Ministry of Foreign Affairs, cable #12, February 5, 1941, JFMDRO, JPF, folder 11.

37. Visas for Ernestyna (no. 478), Gisela (no. 479), and Amelia (no. 480) were unused; all were deported to the Vologda district of the Soviet interior, as were two children, Alexander and Steven.

38. Yamakawa, Acting Secretary (Hamburg) to Iumimero Konoe, cable #6520/#3, March 12, 1941; Consul Akira Yamaji (Vienna) to Foreign Minister Yosuke Matsuoka, #6256/#18, March 10, 1941; Ambassador Hiroshi Oshima (Berlin) to Konoe, #6866 in response to #205, March 15, 1941; Acting

Minister (Stockholm) to Matsuoka, #6384/#27, March 11, 1941; Ambassador Yoshitsugu Tatekawa (Moscow) to Matsuoka, #6561/#292, March 12, 1941, JFMDRO, JPF, folder 11.

39. "The Jewish Community of Kobe, Japan, Committee for Assistance to Refugees [Jewcom] Report, July 1940–November 1941, Kobe, 1942" (hereafter Kobe report), USHMM Collection, Gift of Irene Borovitz and Tamara Rozanski.

40. Pamela Rotner Sakamoto, *Japanese Diplomats and Jewish Refugees: A World War II Dilemma* (Westport, Conn.: Praeger, 1998), 40.

41. Ibid., 56; Foreign Minister Hachiro Arita to Japanese embassies abroad, "Summary of Jewish Policy," cable #3544, December 7, 1938, JFMDRO, JPF, folder 5.

42. "Summary of Jewish Policy."

43. Sakamoto, *Japanese Diplomats,* 56; "Summary of Jewish Policy."

44. Bernhard Kahn, JDC, memorandum of conversation with Kozo Tamura, November 20, 1940, AJJDC Archives, AR 33/44, #723. See also David Kranzler, "Japan Before and During the Holocaust," in *The World Reacts to the Holocaust,* ed. David S. Wyman (Baltimore: Johns Hopkins University Press, 1996), 554–72.

L. P. J. DE DECKER:

1. P. J. [Leendert Pieter Johan] de Decker, Personnel files, Netherlands Ministry of Foreign Affairs Archives, The Hague.

JAN ZWARTENDIJK:

Jan Zwartendijk to Ministry of Foreign Affairs, The Hague, April 9, 1963, Netherlands Ministry of Foreign Affairs Archives, The Hague, file 153.3, "Zwartendijk."

CHIUNE SUGIHARA:

"Gaimusho: Nenkan Ni, 1942" (Foreign Ministry yearbook, 1942) and "Gaimusho Shokuinroku, 1941–42" (Foreign Ministry personnel record, 1940–42), JFMDRO.

Chapter 5: Journey

1. Benjamin Fishoff, "Accompanied by Angels," Meryl Fishoff Private Collection, 3.

2. Sugihara, unpublished report. Between April 17, 1940, and June 2, 1940, Lithuanian and Soviet authorities discussed the transit of refugees through the Soviet Union to Turkey on the way to Palestine, and the Soviets agreed in principle to issuing transit visas to Jewish refugees, contingent upon the issuance of Turkish transit visas (Russian Ministry of Foreign Affairs Archives, Moscow, Historical Documentation Department, AVP RF, f. 0151, op. 31, p. 57, d. 4, l. 15 and p. 58, d. 18, ll. 6–8, 10, 14–16). Turkey was unwilling to grant such visas until late December 1940, according to Zorach Warhaftig (*Refugee and Survivor,* 116).

3. Tadeusz Romer, "The Problem of the Polish Refugees Coming to the Far East," January 15, 1941, Hoover Institution Archives, Stanford, Calif., M.S.Z. Collection, box 526, folder 6, "Refugees," 1941.

4. Fishoff, "Accompanied by Angels," 3.

5. Zuroff, *Response of Orthodox Jewry,* 97.

6. Warhaftig, interview with Levin, 1965.

7. Josef Mlotek, "Autobiography," Lithuanian Central State Archives, Vilnius (hereafter LCSA), f. 757, ap. 8, b. 429, l. 6.

8. David Lifszyc, "Autobiography," LCSA, f. 757, ap. 8, b. 367, l. 5.

9. Fishoff, "Accompanied by Angels," 3.

10. Kahan, *In Fayer un Flamen,* diary entry of January 22, 1941, 255.

11. Glass, interview.

12. Vogelweid, interview.

13. Moses Beckelman, statement to the press, May 21, 1941, AJJDC Archives, Beckelman biographical file, #123B.

14. JDC New York to JDC Lisbon, November 12, 1940, AJJDC Archives, AR 33/44, #732, doc. #8916.

15. JDC Lisbon to JDC New York, November 22, 1940, AJJDC Archives, AR 33/44, #732, doc. #9314.

16. Moses A. Leavitt, "Memorandum on Emigration from Lithuania" (JDC memorandum), January 17, 1941, AJJDC Archives, AR 33/44, #732.

17. Yecheskel Leitner, *Operation: Torah Rescue: The Escape of the Mirrer Yeshiva from War-Torn Poland to Shanghai, China* (Jerusalem and New York: Feldheim Publishers, 1987), 61; Benjamin Gelbfish, videotape interview, June 17, 1999, USHMM, Oral History, RG 50.494, #0008.

18. Fishoff, "Accompanied by Angels," 3.

19. Lithuanian American Information Center, "Appendix A: Classification of 'anti-Soviet' element in Lithuania pursuant to the order of NKVD (People's Commissariat for Internal Affairs) of Soviet Russia," in *An Appeal to Fellow Americans on behalf of the Baltic States by United Organizations of Americans of Lithuanian, Latvian and Estonian Descent* (New York: Lithuanian American Information Center, 1944), 17–28.

20. Ibid.

21. Arad, "Concentration of Refugees," 212.

22. Rabbi Eliezer Silver to Bernard Khan and Moses Leavitt, JDC, January 17, 1941, AJJDC Archives, AR 33/44, #738.

23. H. K. Buchman, "Financial Problem In Re: Lithuanian Emigration" (JDC memorandum), January 8, 1941, AJJDC Archives, AR 33/44, #732, doc. #297.

24. Ibid.

25. Leavitt, "Memorandum on Emigration."

26. Buchman, "Financial Problem."

27. JDC Lisbon to JDC New York, January 9, 1941, AJJDC Archives, AR 33/44, #732.

28. Moses Beckelman to JDC New York, January 17, 1941, AJJDC Archives, AR 33/44, #732.

29. JDC Lisbon to JDC New York, January 2, 1941, AJJDC Archives, AR 33/44, #732, doc. #102.

30. Soltz, *Eight Hundred and Fifty Days,* 71–72.

31. Beckelman, statement to the press, May 21, 1941.

32. Lipschitz, *Shanghai Connection,* 44.

33. Laurence Steinhardt (Moscow) to Cordell Hull, October 6, 1940, NARA, RG 59, entry #704, 811.111, "Refugees," 422.

34. Ibid.

35. Ibid.

36. Giersz Bider, "The Present Situation in Lithuania and J.D.C. Relief Work," December 20, 1940, 4, AJJDC Archives, AR 33/44, #732. Beckelman was meeting with Steinhardt about the problems caused by U.S. policy preventing the transmission of Joint funds from the United States to Lithuania.

37. Glass, interview.

38. Vogelweid, interview.

39. Zlota Ginsburg interview, in Kasnett, *The World That Was: Lithuania*, 97.

40. Romer report, January 15, 1941.

41. Warhaftig, *Refugee and Survivor*, 147; Soltz, *Eight Hundred and Fifty Days*, 96.

42. Soltz, *Eight Hundred and Fifty Days*, 96.

43. Warhaftig, *Refugee and Survivor*, 147.

44. Bider, "The Present Situation in Lithuania."

45. Soltz, *Eight Hundred and Fifty Days*, 99–100.

46. Fishoff, "Accompanied by Angels," 5.

47. Glass, interview.

48. Fishoff, "Accompanied by Angels," 5.

49. Leitner, *Operation: Torah Rescue*, 78–79.

50. Motl Goldberg, videotape interview, August 18, 1999, USHMM, Oral History, RG 50.494, #0017.

51. Oskar Schenker, "For Us the Sun Really Rose in Japan," Alexander Schenker, Private Collection.

52. Kobe report, 8.

53. See the "List[s] of Polish Refugees arrived in Kobe" for the months from January to June 1941, AJJDC Archives, AR 33/44, #726; Sakamoto, *Japanese Diplomats*, 131.

Chapter 6: Stranded

1. Lazar Kahan diary, March 7, 1941, YIVO Institute for Jewish Research, New York City (hereafter YIVO), Rose Shoshana Kahan Archive.

2. Camhi, interview.

3. Kobe report, 16a; Anatole Ponevejsky to JDC New York, February 18, 1941, AJJDC Archives, AR 33/44, #723.

4. Moise Moiseeff, "Situation of the Jewish Refugees in Japan," report to the World Jewish Congress (WJC), June 7, 1941, in *Archives of the Holocaust: The Papers of the World Jewish Congress, 1939–1945*, vol. 8, 159.

5. Soltz, *Eight Hundred and Fifty Days*, 105.

6. J. Epstein, HICEM Kobe, to HICEM Lisbon, August 18, 1941, YIVO, HIAS "Far East," XV/B/24.

7. Moses Leavitt to Joseph Talamo, May 28, 1942; and Henrietta K. Buchman, circular letter, September 3, 1941; AJJDC Archives, AR 33/44, #40-2.

8. Kobe report, 16a.

9. Bluman, interview.

10. Soltz, *Eight Hundred and Fifty Days*, 108.

11. Warhaftig, *Refugee and Survivor*, 161.

12. Ruth Lax, telephone interview with Paul Rose of USHMM, September 12, 1998.

13. Tabuchi Kaneyoshi, *Man, Asahi Camera* (July 1941): 12.

14. Leo Hanin, letter to Rabbi Marvin Tokayer, March 2,

1973, Marvin Tokayer Private Collection.

15. Ibid.

16. Kahan, *In Fayer un Flamen*, diary entry of April 13, 1941, 270.

17. Ibid.

18. Warhaftig, *Refugee and Survivor*, 230.

19. Kahan, *In Fayer un Flamen*, diary entry of June 14, 1941, 277.

20. Sara Arnfeld to Chaim Arnfeld, 1941, USHMM Collection, Gift of Leo Arnfeld.

21. "Vaad Hahatzala," Memorandum prepared by Council of Jewish Federations and Welfare Funds, January 14, 1942, AJJDC Archives, AR 33/44, #362.

22. Register, Lukishki Prison (Vilnius, Lithuania), LCSA, f. R730, ap. 2, b. 35, line #4271.

23. Irene Steinman, telephone interview with Paul Rose of USHMM, June 28, 2000.

24. Jewcom to HICEM Harbin, October 28, 1940, AJJDC Archives, AR 33/44, #723.

25. Notation on Abe Brumberg's identity papers, Abe Brumberg Private Collection.

26. Notation on Abraham Swislocki's identity papers, Norbert Swislocki Private Collection.

27. Kobe report, 9.

28. Anatole Ponevejsky to JDC New York, February 18, 1941, AJJDC Archives, AR 33/44, #723.

29. Kobe report, 9.

30. Leo Hanin, videotape interview, July 7, 1999, USHMM, Oral History, RG 50.494, #0012.

31. Ibid.; Leo Hanin statement, Hoover Institution Archives, Stanford, Calif., Sino-Judaic Collection, Hanin Papers, box 3.

32. Foreign Minister Yosuke Matsuoka to Chiune Sugihara, February 4, 1941, JFMDRO, JPF, folder 11.

33. "Situation of European Refugees Coming to Japan," April 15, 1941, JFMDRO, JPF, folder 11.

34. Japanese Foreign Ministry to Moscow and Vladivostok (Fumumaro Konoe to Saburo Nei), March 19, 1941, JFMDRO, JFP, folder 11.

35. Sakamoto, *Japanese Diplomats*, 147.

36. Fishoff, "Accompanied by Angels," 5.

37. Curaçao list, Royal Netherlands Legation, Tokyo, March 18, 1941, Netherlands Ministry of Foreign Affairs Archives, The Hague, CG Kobe 1918/41, 137.

38. G. N. Zarubin, memorandum of conversation with Sumino, Secretary of the Japanese Embassy in Moscow, April 1, 1941, Russian Ministry of Foreign Affairs Archives, Moscow, Historical Documentation Department, AVP RF, f. 0146, op. 41, p. 227, d. 46, ll. 63–64.

39. A. A. Akudinov, diplomatic agent of the People's Commissariat of Foreign Affairs (NKID) in Vladivostok, secret report of conversation with Japanese Acting Consul Saburo Nei, June 4, 1941, Russian Ministry of Foreign Affairs Archives, Moscow, Historical Documentation Department, AVP RF, f. 0146, op. 41, p. 227, d. 46, l. 108.

40. Sakamoto, *Japanese Diplomats*, 144–47.

41. Kobe report, 22.

42. Moiseeff, "Situation of the Jewish Refugees in Japan," 157.

43. Roy Melbourne, telephone interview with Andrew Campana of USHMM, April 13, 1998.

44. Epstein to HICEM Lisbon, August 18, 1941.

45. Cordell Hull, "To Certain Diplomatic Missions and All Consular Offices Except those in France, Belgium, Netherlands and Germany" (circular memorandum), June 5, 1941, NARA, RG 59, 704, 811.111, "Refugees," 1507.

46. Sondheimer, interview.

47. Moiseeff, "Situation of the Jewish Refugees in Japan," 157.

48. Jechel Lewin to Anatole Ponevejsky, July 9, 1941, USHMM Collection, Gift of Irene Borevitz and Tamara Rozanski.

49. Warhaftig, *Refugee and Survivor*, 211.

50. Ibid., 213.

51. Kobe report, 27.

52. Ibid., 25.

53. Ibid., 27.

54. Epstein to HICEM Kobe, August 18, 1941; Kobe report, 28.

55. Anatole Ponevejsky to N. A. J. de Voogd, February 19, 1941 (misdated February 19, 1940), Netherlands Ministry of Foreign Affairs Archives, The Hague, C. G. Kobe, #137.

56. Anatole Ponevejsky to JDC New York, February 18, 1941, AJJDC Archives, AR 33/44, #723.

57. Kahan, *In Fayer un Flamen*, diary entry of April 13, 1941, 270.

58. Moses Beckelman (Tokyo) to JDC New York, April 1, 1941, AJJDC Archives, AR 33/44, #461, doc. #1677.

59. Warhaftig, *Refugee and Survivor*, 207.

60. Ibid., 205.

61. Meyer Birman to Moses Beckelman, May 8, 1941; "List of recent arrivals," May 2, 1941, AJJDC Archives, AR 33/44, #461.

62. Zuroff, *The Response of Orthodox Jewry*, 163.

63. Jechel Lewin to Anatole Ponevejsky, May 11, 1941, USHMM Collection, Gift of Irene Borevitz and Tamara Rozanski.

64. Jechel Lewin to Anatole Ponevejsky, June 13, 1941, USHMM Collection, Gift of Irene Borevitz and Tamara Rozanski.

65. Jewcom to Anatole Ponevejsky, August 8, 1941, USHMM Collection, Gift of Irene Borevitz and Tamara Rozanski.

66. Hanin, interview.

67. Kobe report, 22–23.

68. Kahan, *In Fayer un Flamen*, diary entry of August 10, 1941, 278.

69. Ibid., diary entry of October 10, 1941, 279.

ANATOLE PONEVEJSKY:

Hanin, interview; "Anatole Ponve Succeeds Factor at Beth El," *B'nai B'rith Messsenger*, February 9, 1962; "A Man Without Peers," *Igud Yotzei Sin in Israel* (Association of Former Residents of China), USHMM Collection, Gift of Irene Borevitz and Tamara Rozanski; Anatole Ponevejsky identity certificate, issued by Hyogo Prefecture, Japan, September 13, 1940, USHMM Collection, Gift of Irene Borevitz and Tamara Rozanski.

TADEUSZ LUDWIG ROMER:

Tadeusz Romer, report of August 31, 1942, Hoover Institution Archives, Stanford, Calif., "Poland," M.S.Z. Collection, box 367, folder 16; List of Polish legation staff from Japan, October 29, 1942, Hoover Institution Archives, "Poland," M.S.Z. Collection, box 368, folder 8; *Nowa encyklopedia powszechna PWN*, 6 vols., s.v. "Romer, Tadeusz" (Warsaw: Wydawnictwo Naukowe PWN, 1995–97), 5:565.

Chapter 7: Exile

1. Vogelweid, interview.

2. Kranzler, *Japanese, Nazis & Jews*, 47.

3. Kahan, *In Fayer un Flamen*, diary entry of October 26, 1941, 283.

4. Swislocki, interview.

5. Ernest Heppner, videotape interview, June 11, 1999, USHMM, Oral History, RG 50.494, #0005.

6. Ernest G. Heppner, *Shanghai Refuge: A Memoir of the World War II Jewish Ghetto* (Lincoln: University of Nebraska Press, 1993), 40–41.

7. Horst Eisfelder, "Exil in China," in *Leben im Wartesaal: Exil in Shanghai, 1938–1947* (Life in the Waiting Room: Exile in Shanghai), ed. Amnon Barzel (Berlin: Jüdisches Museum im Stadtmuseum Berlin, 1997), 85–86, 123.

8. C. Sidney Bertheim to M. A. Leavitt (memorandum), June 26, 1945, AJJDC Archives, AR 33/44, #464.

9. Laura Margolis to Robert Pilpel, May 28, 1941, AJJDC Archives, AR 33/44, #461.

10. Laura Margolis to Robert Pilpel, July 17, 1941, AJJDC Archives, AR 33/44, #461.

11. Meyer Birman, manager of the Far Eastern Central Information Bureau for Immigrants, Shanghai, to HICEM Paris, January 16, 1940, YIVO, HIAS, "Far East," XV/C/6.

12. Margolis to Pilpel, July 17, 1941.

13. Michael Speelman, chairman of the Committee for the Assistance of European Jewish Refugees in Shanghai, to JDC, New York, October 4, 1941, AJJDC Archives, AR 33/44, #462; Joseph R. Fiszman, "The Quest for Status: Polish Jewish Refugees in Shanghai, 1941–1949," *Polish Review* 18, no. 4 (1998): 450.

14. Lipschitz, *Shanghai Connection*, 66.

15. Zlota Ginsburg interview, in Kasnett, *The World That Was: Lithuania*, 102.

16. Sigmund Tobias, *Strange Haven: A Jewish Childhood in Wartime Shanghai* (Urbana and Chicago: University of Illinois Press, 1999), 50.

17. Kahan, *In Fayer un Flamen*, diary entry of December 8, 1941, 289.

18. Goldberg, interview.

19. Yonia Fain, videotape interview, June 6, 1999, USHMM, Oral History, RG 50.494, #0004.

20. Leon Pommers, telephone interview with Paul Rose of USHMM, June 23, 1998.

21. "Jewish Measures in View of the 1942 Situation," January 15, 1942, JFMDRO, JPF, folder 11.

22. Foreign Minister Shigenori Togo, confidential cable to Ambassador Umezu (Manchukuo), Consul Horiuchi

(Shanghai), and Secretary Tsuchikuni (Peking), January 17, 1942, JFMDRO, JPF, folder II.

23. Kranzler, *Japanese, Nazis & Jews,* 455; Fiszman, "The Quest for Status," 450; Bernard Wasserstein, *Secret War in Shanghai: An Untold Story of Espionage, Intrigue, and Treason in World War II* (New York: Houghton Mifflin, 1999), 99–110, 134–40.

24. Vogelweid, interview; Felix Gruenberger, "The Jewish Refugees in Shanghai," *Jewish Social Studies* 12, no. 4 (October 1950): 337–38.

25. Margolis, interview.

26. Laura Margolis, "Race against Time in Shanghai," *Survey Graphic* 33, no. 3 (March 1944): 191.

27. Tobias, *Strange Haven,* 19.

28. Joseph Fiszman to Satu Haase-Webb of USHMM, October 19, 1998.

29. Heppner, *Shanghai Refuge,* 107.

30. Kahan, *In Fayer un Flamen,* diary entry of January 1, 1943, 298.

31. Laura Margolis, "Report of Activities in Shanghai, China, from December 8, 1941, to September 1943," AJJDC Archives, AR 33/44, #463.

32. "Proclamation Concerning Restriction of Residence and Business of Stateless Refugees," *Shanghai Times,* February 18, 1943; Consul-General Seiki Yano (Shanghai) to Minister of Greater East Asia, Kazuo Aoki, "Relocation of Jews," JFMDRO, JPF, folder II.

33. Yano to Aoki, "Relocation of Jews."

34. Jacob Landau, Jewish Telegraphic Agency, New York, reporting on information provided by Isaac Lederman regarding the meeting of Fritz Wiedemann with Japanese officials in Shanghai in 1942, AJJDC Archives, AR 33/44, #463.

35. Hiroshi Oshima (Berlin) to Foreign Minister Shigenori Togo, May 7, 1942, JFMDRO, JPF, folder II.

36. Astrid Freyheisen, *Shanghai und die Politik des Dritten Reiches* (Shanghai and the Politics of the Third Reich) (Würzburg: Königshausen and Neumann, 2000), 458–62.

37. Margolis, "Report of Activities in Shanghai, China."

38. Manuel Siegel to Moses Leavitt, August 26, 1945, AJJDC Archives, AR 33/44, #464; Fain, interview.

39. Polish Residents' Association to Japanese authorities, April 23, 1943, YIVO, Shanghai Collection, RG 243.40.3.

40. Siegel to Leavitt, August 26, 1945; Kahan, *In Fayer un Flamen,* diary entries of May 9, May 12, and May 15, 1944, 312–15; "List of Detained Persons," compiled by a Jewish committee in Shanghai, recording the following individuals as deceased: Artur Seidel (no. 475 on the "Sugihara list"), A. Halperson (no. 370), Beryez Abromowiez (no. 1376), Joseph Altmine (no. 157), Hersz Praszkier (no. 1048), Samuel Haffka (no. 2131), and Theodor Finkelstein (no. 1680), YIVO, RG 243.65.16.

41. Kranzler, *Japanese, Nazis & Jews,* 529–30.

42. Fiszman, "The Quest for Status," 453–54; Gruenberger, "Jewish Refugees," 339, 343.

43. Lipschitz, *Shanghai Connection,* 93.

44. Gruenberger, "Jewish Refugees," 342–43; "Polish Refugees Demand Punishment of Kubota, Okura, Ghoya, and Kano as Chief War Criminals in Shanghai," *Our Life* (Shanghai), September 21, 1945.

45. Mlotek, interview.

46. Joseph Fiszman, interview with Susan Bachrach and Satu Haase-Webb of USHMM, December 18, 1998, Eugene, Oregon.

47. Swislocki, interview.

48. Fain, interview.

49. Kahan, *In Fayer un Flamen,* diary entry of May 10, 1942, 292.

50. Kranzler, *Japanese, Nazis & Jews,* 434.

51. Lipschitz, *Shanghai Connection,* 85.

52. Kranzler, *Japanese, Nazis & Jews,* 427.

53. Sarah Landesman, interview with Tina Lunson of USHMM, May 15, 1998, Silver Spring, Maryland.

54. Heppner, *Shanghai Refuge,* Tobias, *Strange Haven,* Swislocki, interview.

55. C. Brahn to Laura Margolis, April 3, 1944, AJJDC Archives, #463.

56. Kranzler, *Japanese, Nazis & Jews,* 558–60.

57. Zuroff, *Response of Orthodox Jewry,* 211–12.

58. *Our Life* (Shanghai), July 20, 1945; Gruenberger, "Jewish Refugees," 344–45.

59. Gruenberger, "Jewish Refugees," 345.

60. Wasserstein, *Secret War in Shanghai,* 264.

61. Heppner, interview.

62. Nathan Reich to Joseph Hyman, JDC, January 21, 1946, AJJDC Archives, #465.

63. Vogelweid, interview.

64. Gruenberger, "Jewish Refugees," 346.

LAURA MARGOLIS:

Laura Margolis, videotape interview, July 11, 1990, USHMM, Oral History, RG 50.030, #0149.

Remembrance

1. Tobias, *Strange Haven,* 93.

2. Fain, interview.

3. Kahan, *In Fayer un Flamen,* diary entry of September 8, 1945, 354.

"Remembrance" Photographs (pp. 185–199): Lucille Szepsenwol Camhi, New York; Mrs. Zofia Dymant, New York; Joseph Fiszman, Oregon; Rabbi Jacob Ederman, New York; Benjamin Gelbfish, New York; Wanda M. Glass, New York; Morton Goldberg, New York; Nathan Gutwirth, Belgium; USHMM, Gift of Rebeka Ilutovich; David Kirszencwejg, New York; Sarah Landesman, Maryland; Markus Nowogrodzki, New York; USHMM, Gift of Irene Rothenberg; Ruth Berkowicz Segal, New Hampshire; Leo Melamed, Illinois; The Family of Rabbi David and Zipporah Lifshitz, New York; The Family of Abraham Zalcgendler, New York; USHMM, Gift of Leo Arnfeld; Rabbi Moshe Zupnik, New York

Abella, Irving, and Harold Troper. *None Is Too Many: Canada and the Jews of Europe, 1933–1948.* New York: Random House, 1983.

Arad, Yitzhak. "Concentration of Refugees in Vilna on the Eve of the Holocaust." *Yad Vashem Studies on the European Jewish Catastrophe and Resistance* 9, ed. Livia Rothkirchen (1973): 201–15.

———. *Ghetto in Flames: The Struggle and Destruction of Jews in Vilna in the Holocaust.* New York: Holocaust Library, 1982.

Bauer, Yehuda. *American Jewry and the Holocaust: The American Jewish Joint Distribution Committee, 1933–1945.* Detroit: Wayne State University Press, 1981.

———. "Rescue Operations through Vilna." *Yad Vashem Studies on the European Jewish Catastrophe and Resistance* 9, ed. Livia Rothkirchen (1973): 215–25.

Begin, Menachem. *White Nights: The Story of a Prisoner in Russia.* Translated by Katie Kaplan. New York: Harper & Row, 1957, 1977.

Breitman, Richard, and Alan M. Kraut. *American Refugee Policy and European Jewry 1933–1945.* Bloomington: Indiana University Press, 1987.

Bunim, Amos. *A Fire in His Soul: Irving Bunim 1901–1980, the Man and His Impact on American Orthodox Jewry.* Jerusalem and New York: Feldheim Publishers, 1989.

Crowe, David. *The Baltic States and the Great Powers: Foreign Relations, 1938–1940.* Boulder, Colo.: Westview Press, 1993.

Dicker, Herman. *Wanderers and Settlers in the Far East: A Century of Jewish Life in China and Japan.* New York: Twayne Publishers, Inc., 1962.

Feingold, Henry L. *The Politics of Rescue: The Roosevelt Administration and the Holocaust, 1938–1945.* New York: Holocaust Library, 1970.

Ganor, Solly. *Light One Candle: A Survivor's Story of Holocaust Demons and Japanese Heroes.* New York: Kodansha International, 1995.

Goodman, David G., and Masanori Miyazawa. *Jews in the Japanese Mind: The History and Uses of a Cultural Stereotype.* New York: The Free Press, 1995.

Greenbaum, Masha. *The Jews of Lithuania.* Jerusalem: Geffen Publishing, 1995.

Gross, Jan T. *Revolution from Abroad: The Soviet Conquest of Poland's Western Ukraine and Western Belorussia.* Princeton: Princeton University Press, 1988.

Guang, Pan, ed. *The Jews of Shanghai.* Shanghai: Shanghai Pictorial Publishing House, 1995.

Gutman, Yisrael. "Jews in General Anders' Army in the Soviet Union." *Yad Vashem Studies on the European Jewish Catastrophe and Resistance* 12 (1977): 231–96.

———. *Jews of Warsaw, 1939–43: Ghetto, Underground, Revolt.* Translated by Ina Friedman. Bloomington: Indiana University Press, 1982.

Heppner, Ernest G. *Shanghai Refuge: A Memoir of the World War II Jewish Ghetto.* Lincoln: University of Nebraska Press, 1993.

Hirszowicz, Lukasz. "NKVD Documents Shed New Light on Fate of Erlich and Alter." *East European Jewish Affairs* 22, no. 2 (Winter 1992): 65–85.

Kasnett, Yitzhak. *The World That Was: Lithuania.* Cleveland Heights, Ohio: Hebrew Academy of Cleveland, 1996.

Kranzler, David. *Japanese, Nazis & Jews: The Jewish Refugee Community of Shanghai, 1938–1945.* Hoboken, N.J.: KTAV Publishing House, Inc., 1988.

———. "Japan Before and During the Holocaust." In *The World Reacts to the Holocaust,* edited by David S. Wyman, 554–72. Baltimore: Johns Hopkins University Press, 1996.

Krasno, Rena. *Strangers Always: A Jewish Family in Wartime Shanghai.* Berkeley: Pacific View Press, 1992.

Leitner, Yecheskel. *Operation: Torah Rescue: The Escape of the Mirrer Yeshiva from War-Torn Poland to Shanghai, China.* Jerusalem and New York: Feldheim Publishers, 1987.

Levin, Dov. "The Attitude of the Soviet Union to the Rescue of the Jews." In *Rescue Attempts during the Holocaust,* edited by Yisrael Gutman and Efraim Zuroff, 225–46. Jerusalem: Yad Vashem, 1977.

———. *The Lesser of Two Evils: Eastern European Jewry under Soviet Rule, 1939–1941.* Philadelphia: The Jewish Publication Society, 1995.

———. "Lithuanian Jewish Refugees in the Soviet Union during World War II, 1941–45." *Studies in Contemporary Jewry* 4 (1988): 185–209.

Levine, Hillel. *In Search of Sugihara: The Elusive Japanese Diplomat Who Risked His Life to Rescue 10,000 Jews from the Holocaust.* New York: The Free Press, 1996.

Lewin, Isaac. *Remember the Days of Old: Historical Essays.* New York: Research Institute of Religious Jewry, Inc., 1994.

Lincoln, Anna. *Escape to China.* Woodhaven, N.Y.: Manyland Books, Inc., 1982.

Lipschitz, Chaim. *The Shanghai Connection.* New York: Maznaim Publishing Co., 1988.

Melamed, Leo (with Bob Tamarkin). *Escape to the Futures.* New York: John Wiley & Sons, 1996.

Mowrer, Lilian T. *Arrest and Exile.* New York: William Morrow & Company, 1941.

Ofer, Dalia. *Escaping the Holocaust: Illegal Immigration to the Land of Israel 1939–1944.* New York: Oxford University Press, 1990.

Palasz-Rutkowska, Ewa, and Andrzej T. Romer. "Polish-Japanese Co-operation during World War II." *Japan Forum* 7, no. 2 (Autumn 1995): 285–316.

Rakefett-Rothkoff, Aaron. *The Silver Era in American Jewish Orthodoxy.* New York: Yeshiva University Press, 1981.

Rubin, Evelyn Pike. *Ghetto Shanghai*. New York: Shengold Press, 1993.

Sakamoto, Pamela Rotner. *Japanese Diplomats and Jewish Refugees: A World War II Dilemma*. Westport, Conn.: Praeger, 1998.

Soltz, Shmuel. *Eight Hundred and Fifty Days from Border to Border during the Second World War*. Givatayim, Israel: Shmuel Soltz, 1988.

Sugihara, Yukiko. *Visas for Life*. Translated by Hiroki Sugihara. San Francisco: Edu-Comm Plus, 1995.

Sword, Keith. *Deportation and Exile: Poles in the Soviet Union, 1939–48*. New York: St. Martin's Press, 1994.

Tobias, Sigmund. *Strange Haven: A Jewish Childhood in Wartime Shanghai*. Urbana and Chicago: University of Illinois Press, 1999.

Tokayer, Marvin, and Mary Swartz. *The Fugu Plan: The Untold Story of the Japanese and the Jews during World War Two*. New York: Weatherhill, Inc., 1979.

United States Holocaust Memorial Museum. *Hidden History of the Kovno Ghetto*. Boston: Bulfinch Press, 1997.

Warhaftig, Zorach. *Refugee and Survivor: Rescue Efforts during the Holocaust*. Translated by Avner Tomaschoff. Jerusalem: Yad Vashem, 1988.

Wasserstein, Bernard. *Secret War in Shanghai: An Untold Story of Espionage, Intrigue, and Treason in World War II*. New York: Houghton Mifflin, 1999.

Weinberg, Robert. *Stalin's Forgotten Zion: Birobidzhan and the Making of a Soviet Jewish Homeland*. Berkeley: University of California Press, 1998.

Wyman, David S. *Paper Walls: America and the Refugee Crisis 1938–1941*. Amherst: University of Massachusetts Press, 1968.

Zuroff, Efraim. *The Response of Orthodox Jewry in the United States to the Holocaust: The Activities of the Vaad ha-Hatzala Rescue Committee, 1939–1945*. New York: Michael Scharf Publication Trust of the Yeshiva University Press, 2000.

INDEX

"We felt that we lost everything we ever knew.

But at the same time we felt that our life was a gift

because it was a miracle—an accident.

We tried not to struggle with the question,

'Why do I deserve to be alive when my brothers died,

when my family died?'"

—YONIA FAIN

Jaca Hersz-Perzich

2 1180

Le Consulat des Pays-Bas à
Kaunas déclare par la présente
que pour l'admission d'étrangers
au Surinam, au Curaçao
et autres possessions néerlandaises en Amérique
un visa d'entrée n'est pas
requis.

Kaunas, le 27 juillet 1940

L. Zwartendijk

Consul des Pays-Bas à
Kaunas

TRANSIT. VISA.

Seen for the journey
through Japan (to Suranam,
Curaçao and other Nether-
lands' colonies.)
1940 VII. 31.

Consul du Japon à Kaunas.

國許可
署第202號
出國期限
昭和16年8月23日
經由
神戸
上海

過過特許
昭和16年3月14日
ヨリ向フ十四日間有効
福井縣

入國特許
自昭和16 3月28日
至昭和16 5月26日
兵庫縣

右名ハ行先地ノ査証ヲ有スルモ日本帝国ヲ通過
スルニ必要ナル現金ヲ持セス且ツ乗船券ノ
予約ナキモ本人ニ付キ在神戸猶太人協會
ノ保証ヲ徴シ通過 特許セリ

BRITISH CONSULATE SHANGHAI
Passport Control Office

CONSULAT DU JAPON
KAUNAS. LITHUANIE
大日本帝國領事館之印

REQUIRED TO REPORT TO
ALIENS DEPARTMENT
ELL BAZAR, CALCUTTA
IN 24 HOURS SHROH
DATE

TRANSIT. VISA.

Seen for the journey
through Japan (to Suranam,
Curaçao and other Nether-
lands' colonies.)
1940. VII. 31.

Consul du Japon à Kaunas.

CONSULAT DU JAPON
KAUNAS. LITHUANIE

British Consulate General Shanghai
Passport Control Officer

September, 1941. 16
Shanghai
Pr. G. E. A. Gardner

出國許可
署第202號

出國期限
昭和16年8月23日

線
神戸線
經由向
上海
兵庫

出國特許
自昭和16 3 28日
至昭和16 5 26日
兵庫縣

福井県

其者ハ行先地ノ査証ヲ有スルニ本籍通過
ニ必要ナル現金ヲ有セシ且ツ乗船券ノ
ヲ約シヤキ者ニ付キ在神戸猶太人協會
ノ保証ヲ徴シ通過
特許セリ

REQUIRED TO REPORT TO
ALIENS DEPARTMENT
BAZAR, CALCUTTA
WITHIN 24 HOURS
DATE